M000286915

Human Resource Management for Golf Course Superintendents

Robert A. Milligan, Ph.D
Thomas R. Maloney
Cornell University

WILEY

JOHN WILEY & SONS, INC.

Library of Congress Cataloging-in-Publication Data:

ISBN: 1-57504-038-7

10 9 8 7

Acknowledgments

The authors are grateful to many people for their support, assistance, and contributions to this book. First, this book would not have been possible without the interest, support, and guidance of the Golf Course Superintendents Association of America. GCSAA staff members were instrumental in guiding us through many months of writing, reviews, and edits of book chapters.

During the early stages of writing we met with the GCSAA Magazine Committee twice. Committee members provided valuable perspectives on the day-to-day operation of the golf course maintenance staff and provided many practical insights and examples which we have drawn upon throughout the book.

We have also interacted individually with a number of golf course superintendents. Four superintendents who deserve special recognition are: Tony Brown, The Country Club of Charleston, Charleston, SC; Thomas Charnock, CGCS Brookfield Country Club, Clarence, NY; Bruce Peeples, Spring Lake Golf Club, Spring Lake, NJ; and Gregory J. Wojick, CGCS Greenwich Country Club, Greenwich, CT. We are very grateful to them for their support and assistance, and insights into their profession.

Our professional colleagues at Cornell University and Cornell Cooperative Extension have provided a great deal of support, encouragement, and influence on our work. Dr. William Tomek, our department chairman at the time the book was proposed, provided his wholehearted support and encouragement. Guy Hutt worked with us in developing much of the material that served as a basis for the book. We are very grateful for the opportunity to work with and learn from him. Jonas Kauffman and Beth Claypoole were also instrumental in developing aspects of the material used in writing the book.

We are also grateful for the support and influence we have received from Dr. Bernard Erven, Professor of Farm Management at The Ohio State University. The opportunity to collaborate with Bernie during a sabbatical at Cornell as well as in subsequent years has expanded our human resource management outlook and has challenged our thinking. His influence, too, is an important part of this book.

During the course of writing, three Cornell communication students were hired to provide research and editorial assistance. They are Amy Bibbens, Kate Reynolds, and Kristine Petracek. We are extremely grateful to each of them for their editorial assistance and expertise, their research, their helpful suggestions, and most of all, their patience.

Our secretarial staff has been dedicated, supportive, and patient throughout the process. Secretaries instrumental in typing, updating, and proofing the manuscript include: Beverly Carcelli, Cindy Farrell, and Judy Neno. Each has our sincere thanks.

Contents

A Human Resource Approach To Management

A Tale of Two Golf Courses

This is a story about two country clubs near each other in the suburbs of a small city. The two are similar by all outward appearances. Both have attractive, well-maintained clubhouses and are led by a general manager, a board of directors, and a green committee that oversees the work of the golf course superintendent. Each club has a well-designed, 18-hole golf course about 40 years old. Both golf courses have the same soil type and modern equipment. While the physical resources of both clubs are alike, the underlying personnel issues are different.

Jim Lewis, the superintendent at the Successful Valley Country Club, has a reputation for excellence in golf course management. Recently he hired a bright young assistant superintendent and together they manage a crew of two year-round workers and ten seasonal workers. The relationship between Jim and his assistant manager is based on teamwork and mutual respect. They work well together, and Jim always delegates responsibility as soon as his assistant is ready to accept it. The golf course crew, which consists mostly of college students, is a hard-working, committed team. They understand their jobs and properly operate each piece of equipment. The staff exhibits high morale and a feeling of camaraderie.

Jim, his assistant, and the entire crew work toward a common goal: to maintain the course in tournament condition for as much of the golfing season as possible, given the weather and other external constraints. They are successful in achieving that objective and the course has a reputation for being one of the finest in the area.

Not only does Jim have an excellent crew, but he also has managed—sometimes under difficult conditions—to maintain excellent working relationships with the general manager, key representatives on the board of directors, and the green committee. In the past when Jim has fought for financial resources or policy changes to manage the course more effectively, he usually has had his requests approved.

Bob Ryan, golf course superintendent at the Low Life Country Club, has had far less success than his colleague Jim Lewis. Every time Bob thinks things are going well, something seems to go wrong; he doesn't understand it. He works harder than anyone he knows, averaging 75 to 80 hours per week during the season. Bob also has an assistant golf course superintendent and a crew of about a dozen people, several of whom are year-round employees. Most of the employees are intelligent and capable of getting the job done, if they would just stop squabbling and apply themselves. In the last few years, turnover among the golf course crew has been very high. It is rare for a third of the crew to stay an entire season. Equipment often is improperly adjusted and seems to break a lot. Bob is constantly lecturing the crew on the importance of proper maintenance. He never finds the time, however, to train successfully any one individual before he is called off to another "crisis."

Bob's greatest strength is his ability to grow and maintain excellent greens and fairways. He graduated at the top of his class from one of the finest horticultural schools in the country. He worked on golf courses each summer during high school and college. His technical knowledge of turfgrass maintenance and production is outstanding. Yet, trying to achieve a tournament-condition course, even for the biggest tournament of the year, seems to be an impossible dream for Bob and his crew. The assistant superintendent asks Bob to make lists of long- and short-term jobs that need to be done, but Bob is always so busy solving problems out on the course that there is never time for more than five or ten minutes of planning.

Turmoil and frustration characterize Bob's relationships with committee members. The green committee chairman visits Bob's office frequently during the golf season. He constantly brings Bob complaints about fairway maintenance, turf disease, insect problems, and the inappropriate behavior of his crew. Originally Bob had a performance review once a year, but recently the green committee voted to review Bob's performance four times a year in hopes of correcting the problems with the course.

The biggest tournament of the year is three weeks away, yet staff morale is at an all-time low, and the green committee members' concern has never been greater. Bob is extremely frustrated and seriously thinking of quitting his job. He doesn't understand how someone who graduated at the top of his college class and has such extensive knowledge of golf course maintenance could have all these problems.

* * *

Most real-life golf course situations lie somewhere between these fictitious extremes. These examples, however, highlight two important points. First, a well-managed organization and an effectively supervised staff are no accident. Effective organizations grow out of a commitment to proper management and an interest in building a successful organization.

Second, management skills are not innate, but learned. People are not born with the ability to properly train a new worker, to counsel an employee with a problem, or to discipline an employee. Somewhere in the past, the effective manager has learned proper management and supervisory skills. A large part of the problem in the case above is that while he is an expert at turf care and maintenance, Bob never mastered the management skills necessary to deal with the people on the green committee and on his staff. In short, Bob is a very good "doer," but a poor manager. Management can be learned and improved over time through education, mentoring, and on-the-job experience. Superintendents who view management education as a process of growth and development throughout their careers have the greatest opportunity to achieve management excellence and to develop an organization that rivals the Successful Valley Country Club.

It is wrong to think that there is a magic formula for effective management; there is not. This book takes a practical approach to managing a golf course and its personnel. It draws on decades of research and study in the fields of management science, human resource management, psychology, organizational behavior, and organizational development. It describes how these principles work and applies them to situations that golf course superintendents face every day. The purpose of this book is to provide golf course superintendents and assistant superintendents with the tools necessary to develop a satisfied, productive workforce—one that will work with you to meet the mission and objectives of the golf course whether you work for a country club, a municipal golf course, or yourself.

The Golf Course Superintendent as a Manager

Operating a golf course is a complex job. Many golf course managers have training only in the production or technical turfgrass management aspects of their job. This is the area where they feel comfortable. Successful operation of the course, however, requires that the manager master both the production and the personnel management components of the job.

Management science has evolved over the past century to become a broadly defined discipline with many interrelated parts. We offer the following definition of management: **Management is determining what must be done and achieving desired results through one's own efforts and the efforts of other people.**

What does this mean to the golf course superintendent? To successfully maintain a golf course, like that at the Successful Valley Country Club, it means the golf course superintendent must have both turf production expertise and management expertise. Further, just as recommended turf production practices are based on research principles from ongoing university and industry studies, the management principles and practices in this book are based on management science research and are used every day in successful businesses and organizations, including golf courses.

The framework for this book follows the "management process" school of management, which originates from the pioneering work of Henri Fayol in the early 1900s. Fayol introduced the systematic study of management through the recognition that it involves more than technical operations (Fayol, 1929). This recognition led to the identification of the manager's activities or functions; we can think of them as the job description of the manager. In this book we include five functions: planning, organizing, controlling, staffing, and directing.

Before Fayol's interpretation, management teaching and application centered on developing the most scientific, rational principles for handling the inputs of production: machines, materials, people, and money. Today management analysts, operations researchers, and systems analysts continue this focus with their emphasis on decisionmaking and optimal use of business resources.

Fayol's recognition that people have a unique role in the process led to research focusing on human behavior and interpersonal interactions. The resulting principles and practices—based in psychology, sociology, anthropology, and other behavioral sciences—are an important part of the golf course superintendent's role as supervisor and leader.

Most managers of small businesses and organizations, like golf courses, have their training in production. It is natural that they, like the early management scientists, view people primarily as inputs into production. As successful managers gain management expertise, they recognize that the manager has many functions, including promoting the development of people in the organization. The manager of the Low Life Country Club has not made this transition. In this book we lead you systematically through the five functions of management while focusing primarily on the supervision and development of people within your organization.

Figure 1.1 illustrates the framework from which this book is written. It includes five interrelated functions and reflects the importance of planning. This illustration recognizes that planning is central to the functions of organizing, controlling, staffing, and directing.

The Functions of Management

Now that we have discussed the role of the golf course superintendent as manager, let's look specifically at each management function.

Figure 1.1.

1. Planning

Planning is the process of providing direction for the organization. The planning process has several parts, including developing a vision and a mission, determining goals, developing short- and long-term plans to reach goals, preparing tactics to implement the plan, and putting in place follow-up procedures to make changes when necessary. In short, the planning process creates a vision for what is to be accomplished (Catt and Miller, 1991).

2. Organizing

The organizing function involves grouping the tasks to be done and then assigning appropriate individuals or groups to accomplish those tasks. The organizational structure, lines of authority within that structure (who reports to whom), and channels of communication usually are communicated by a written organizational chart.

3. Controlling

The controlling function is the process of determining how well the actual performance of the organization relates to the plans and goals that have been developed. This process includes creating performance standards, measuring performance, and making corrections as necessary to achieve desired results.

4. Staffing

The staffing function is strongly related to the human resource functions that are typically associated with the personnel department in a large company. Staffing directly relates to hiring productive individuals and developing them to achieve the mission and goals of the organization. This function includes recruitment, selection, training, and performance appraisal. In small organizations without personnel departments, the manager must assume these responsibilities.

5. Directing

The directing function is the process of giving directions and guiding the work of the individuals within the organization. Directing requires the manager to have a variety of supervisory skills that ensure that employees complete assigned work activities. Directing activities include leadership, motivation, communication, and discipline (Catt and Miller, 1991).

While this book is based on all five functions of management, we focus heavily on two functions: staffing and directing. Figure 1.2 builds on the five functions of management previously discussed by identifying specific activities within the staffing and directing function. This figure provides the framework for each chapter of this book. Chapters 2–4 focus on the management functions of planning, organizing, and controlling. The remaining chapters focus on specific topics included in the staffing and directing management functions.

The Plan of This Book

This book is based on two basic assumptions. First, every manager in a small organization, such as a golf course or a country club, engages in each of the five management functions outlined. Therefore, each management function is addressed. Second, since the functions of staffing and directing are most closely related to Human Resource Management, these two functions are addressed in detail. The following is a brief description of each chapter.

Part I—A Framework for Management

Chapter 1—A Human Resource Approach to Management

Explanation of the management base from which the book is written.

Figure 1.2

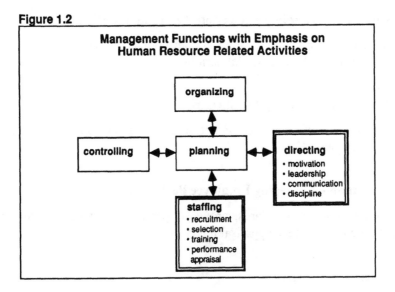

Chapter 2—The Superintendent as a Planner

What the manager needs to know about long- and short-term planning in order to effectively lead the organization.

Chapter 3—Organizational Structure

A hierarchical plan for all individuals within the organization to provide structure within the business.

Chapter 4—Controlling to Ensure Goal Achievement

Control concepts, such as measuring performance, that are necessary to achieve the organization's objectives.

Part II—Staffing

This section is aimed at providing the manager with the necessary tools to ensure that highly qualified individuals are attracted to the organization, that they are trained and developed effectively, and that their performance is monitored and evaluated on a regular basis.

Chapter 5—Employee Recruitment: Attracting Qualified Applicants

Recruiting the most qualified applicants for available positions.

Chapter 6—Employee Selection: Choosing the Right Person

Choosing the most qualified applicant. Selection activities include interviewing, reference checking, and trial periods.

Chapter 7—Training for Success

Orientation for new employees, and personal career development and training for all employees.

Chapter 8—Managing Employee Performance

Setting performance standards, providing performance feedback, and conducting the performance appraisal interview.

Part III—Directing

This section focuses on the directing function of management. The directing function involves supervisory skills including motivation, leadership, communication, and discipline.

Chapter 9—Leadership

A variety of leadership qualities and concepts, including the use of power, leadership styles, and situational leadership.

Chapter 10—Employee Motivation

Applying motivation theory and practical principles of supervision to motivate the workforce.

Chapter 11—The Golf Course Superintendent as a Communicator

Essential communication skills and tools for effective personnel management and conflict resolution techniques.

Chapter 12—Employee Discipline and Discharge

Using discipline and discharge in a constructive way to correct unacceptable employee performance and maintain the integrity of the organization.

Chapter 13—Total Quality in Golf Course Management

Weaving together the principles of management into a total quality framework that focuses on satisfying the golfer as the ultimate customer.

We have also included **"Key Points"** in every chapter. These serve as a good preview of information in the upcoming section, and are also helpful for review purposes. In addition, they can be useful for finding information quickly. Take advantage of the Key Points to make this book more useful to you in your management role.

A Human Resource Focus

Human resource management in organizations has its roots in management science and in the five functions of management previously described. Managing people effectively is like conducting an orchestra. All individuals in the organization must understand their roles, be trained to perform them, and work effectively as a team. In the case of an orchestra, the end result is a harmonious work of music. In the case of a golf course, the end result is a carefully managed and manicured course that the staff and golfers can be proud of.

The superintendent's job is often referred to as golf course management. In reality the superintendent's job is not managing the course, but managing the people who maintain the course. As indicated earlier, good human resource managers are not born. They learn their management skills over time through constant effort and attention. Managers who seek to improve their skills must recognize the need to change their own behavior when dealing with people in order to become better human resource managers. This shift is not easy. It takes courage to recognize the changes necessary, experiment with new human resource management practices and constantly practice sound management skills. The road to management excellence will have obstacles, but those who invest the time and effort will discover the benefits as their management responsibilities and successes grow.

The field of modern human resource management provides the principles and practices needed to become better managers of people. Figure 1.3 summarizes the characteristics of companies with both effective and ineffective human resource management practices. The conclusions summarized in this table are the results of a survey of 785 opinion leaders or individuals presumed to have well-informed perspectives on current human resource management practices in American businesses. The telephone survey, conducted by the IBM Corporation, attempted to assess current policies and practices of human resource professionals and related individuals. The characteristics of effective companies outlined in Figure 1.3, such as concern

Figure 1.3. Effective vs. Ineffective Human Resource Practices

Characteristics of Effective Companies	Characteristics of Ineffective Companies
• Have genuine concern for people and a positive view of employees as assets	• Do not view employees as important assets; show little concern for workforce
• Offer adequate training, development, and advancement opportunities	• Offer little or no employee development and an ineffective internal advancement process
• Retain employees; have low turnover	• See high employee turnover
• Have open internal communication	• Exhibit poor internal communication
• Feature top management commitment and support of human resources	• Manage in an autocratic or bureaucratic manner
• Pay well; offer suitable compensation programs	• Have unclear or outdated policies, inconsistently administered and changed to suit management needs
• Encourage employee participation	

Adapted from: S.W. Alper and R.E. Mandel. 1984. *What Policies and Practices Characterize the Most Effective HR Departments? Personnel Administrator* 29 No. 11:120–24.

for individuals as valuable assets, training, development, and adequate compensation, are emphasized throughout the book. Superintendents seeking to improve their management skills should strive for these goals. You likely will learn about management techniques that are quite different and sometimes more time-consuming than the ones you are now using. Carefully studied and correctly implemented, these practices will provide the cornerstone for achieving your golf course's vision and goals as well as your own.

Summary

The primary function of a golf course superintendent is to utilize all the available resources to create the best golf course possible. In this book we take a modern approach to Human Resource Management, viewing people as the most important asset in golf course management. The principles and practices described in the chapters ahead are designed to help you bring out the **best** performance golf course employees have to offer.

The five functions of management—**planning** and providing direction for the organization, **organizing** and assigning work to be done, **controlling** and monitoring the success of the organization, **staffing** the organization and developing those employees, and **directing** and guiding the work of the organization—are effective tools in proper management of any organization. We encourage you to examine your leadership and supervisory skills and identify areas where you can personally grow and improve. Work on developing traits of successful human resource managers, including viewing employees as valued assets, providing development opportunities and strong compensation programs for employees, encouraging employee participation, and offering open communication with employees.

We also encourage you to use these skills to create a work environment where employees can become peak performers. With the appropriate amount of effort, the payoff can be tremendous: improved employee morale, increased commitment to golf course goals, outstanding performance, and reduced management stress.

References

Alper, S.W. and R.E. Mandel. 1981. What policies and practices characterize the most effective HR departments? Personnel Administrator 29(11):120–124.

Catt, S.E. and D.S. Miller. 1991. Supervision working with people. 2nd ed. Richard D. Irwin Inc., Homewood, IL.

Cox, D. 1992. Leadership when the heat's on. McGraw-Hill, Inc., New York.

Fayol, H. 1929. Industrial and general administration, translated by J.A. Coubrough. International Management Institute, Geneva, Switzerland.

Harwell, E.M. 1985. The complete manager. Chain Store Publishing Corporation, New York.

Heneman, H.G., III, D.P. Schwab, J.A. Fossum, and L.D. Dyer. 1986. Personnel/Human resource management. 3rd ed. Richard D. Irwin, Inc., Homewood, IL.

Hodgetts, R.M. 1986. Management: Theory, process, and practice. 4th ed. Academic Press Inc., Orlando, FL.

Miles, R.E. 1963. Human relations or human resources. Harvard Business Review, July–August.

Milligan, R.A. and G.K. Hutt. 1989. A conceptual and operational framework for teaching management to farm managers. A.E. Staff Paper No. 89-27, August.

2

The Superintendent as a Planner

In contrasting the Successful Valley Country Club and the Low Life Country Club in Chapter 1, it was concluded that Jim Lewis excelled in managing the golf course personnel at the Successful Valley Country Club. Jim, like most golf course superintendents, is most comfortable working on the golf course. Jim also recognizes that most of the work on the golf course is completed by the people he supervises. His success, therefore, is determined primarily by how effectively the staff carries out the plans developed with his leadership.

Your biggest barrier to effective management, especially during the busiest times, can be the desire to function as part of the golf course maintenance staff. The technical golf course work, after all, is what everyone is striving to accomplish, and perhaps is what you enjoy most about your job. The success of the golf course, however, depends more on your ability to effectively manage the employees you supervise. Effective planning through goal setting makes this management possible.

As a planner, the golf course superintendent must provide the leadership to develop the vision, mission, goals, and tactics to enable the golf course staff to efficiently and enthusiastically do their job (Figure 2.1). The vision and mission serve as the basis for planning. Establishing vision and mission requires that the superintendent work with other leaders of the golf club. Once established, the vision and mission provide the basis for developing goals and tactics for maintenance of the golf course. This chapter first considers the establishment of the vision and mission for the golf club or course. The next sections address the key role and potential of goal setting, and the use of tactical planning to ensure goal achievement. Goal setting and tactical planning are tools to support the vision and mission.

Figure 2.1

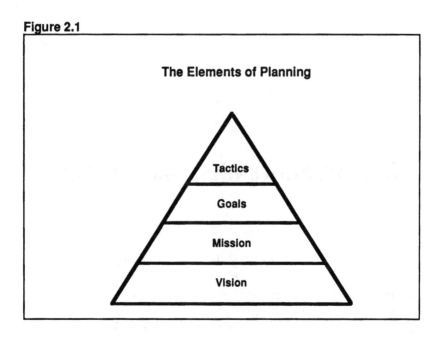

The Elements of Planning

(pyramid diagram, top to bottom: Tactics, Goals, Mission, Vision)

Establishing Vision and Mission

Key Points
- Development of leadership's vision for the golf club is essential to peak performance.
- A mission statement articulates that vision.
- All course personnel should have ownership of the mission.

The golf course superintendent is only one of those involved in establishing the vision for the golf club. Others (depending on the course's organization) include the owner, the golf professional, the club manager, the board of directors, the green committee, and the membership. Communication and consensus building among these leaders about their vision for the club is essential, though obtaining consensus is never easy. Including the membership at private courses and involvement of local bureaucrats at municipal courses adds complexity. Although these complexities are difficult to deal with, they enhance the importance of establishing a vision. Consensus on the vision is a necessity.

The vision focuses on where the golf club hopes to be in the future. Components of the vision include the size and layout of the course, the number and makeup of the golfers, the magnitude and character of the services provided, and the capabilities of the employees. It is imperative that all managers—including golf course superintendents, golf professionals, and general managers—work with the membership and the owner(s) or public officials in reaching consensus for the vision. If top management cannot agree to and commit to the vision, how can they gain commitment from personnel working for the course? It is also crucial that the vision for the future of the club or course be a highly visible component of recruitment and selection. Once consensus is reached, a mission statement for the club should be developed that embodies that vision.

The mission statement should describe the vision for the club or course and also include the principles and guiding values integral to attaining the vision. A club could have a vision of improving the course to be the best in the region and attracting a PGA event. The values of being member friendly, environmentally responsible, and diverse in membership must also be included in the mission.

Everyone connected with the golf club—managers, members, public officials, employees, and suppliers—should be committed to the club's mission. If your club or course does not have a mission statement, commitment can be gained by involving everyone in developing a mission statement. Where commitment to the current mission exists, new employees and members must be oriented to the mission; it must be a key part of recruitment and orientation. The process of developing or refining vision and mission is not easy. In cases where managers are having difficulty establishing a vision and mission, it may be appropriate to utilize the services of a management consultant.

Developing the Mission Statement

The mission statement should explain why the golf course exists, based on the shared vision, which reflects the values and beliefs of the course managers, the members or advisers, and the employees. The mission statement describes what services are to be offered at the club, and their purpose. One course, for example, may see its mission as enabling all golfers to reach their absolute potential at golf. Another club may view its mission as providing the ultimate opportunity for relaxation from life's pressures. A third club may view its mission as primarily social.

The mission should also describe the culture of the club and the benefits to all stakeholders of the club. How important is it that members and employees relate to each other? Should the atmosphere be oriented toward seriousness or fun? Is employee growth and advancement important? Is the emphasis on attracting new golfers or serving the current members?

The following four questions need to be answered when articulating the mission statement for the course:

1. What is the golf club in operation to do? What are the services offered and the purpose of the course?
2. What would we like the golf club to be? This includes its position in the industry and the community, its strengths, and its physical qualities.
3. What values do we choose as a foundation for our course? What do we want others to say about our golf club?
4. What should the course contribute to each stakeholder (leaders, golfers, employees, and suppliers)?

Covey, Merrill, and Merrill (1994; p. 222) include the following six items as characteristics of an empowering mission statement:

- *"It focuses on contributions, or worthwhile purposes that create a collective deep burning 'Yes.'"* The mission statement should provide a focus to rally around. It is written to reflect people's feelings and values; it is not a literary piece for others to read. It should provide meaning to the job.

- *"It comes from the bowels of the organization, not from Mount Olympus."* Whether involved in the development or not, everyone involved in the golf course must feel they are an important part of attaining the mission. A mission is not something that is inflicted upon people.

- *"It is based on timeless principles."* The mission must be a "compass" or central focus that guides the club through good times and bad. This "compass" should serve as a guide for action at times when inaction or justifications based on "it's not my job" would be detrimental.

- *"It contains both vision and principle-based values."* The mission statement embodies the vision and the values (hard work, honesty, integrity, social awareness, etc.) to be considered in reaching the vision.

- *"It addresses the needs of all stakeholders."* A stakeholder is anyone impacted by the success or failure of the organization. They include golfers, neighbors, suppliers, and employees.

- *"It addresses all four needs and capacities."* The four are the physical/economic ("to live"), the social/emotional ("to love"), the psychological need to use and develop our individual capabilities ("to learn"), and the spiritual, or need for meaning in one's work ("to leave a legacy").

Your golf club may or may not have a mission statement. In either case you should develop a golf course maintenance mission statement. If the club has a mission statement, the golf course maintenance mission statement must be consistent with it while relating directly to the maintenance of the course and the personnel dedicated to that task. If the club has no mission statement, you need to provide the leadership necessary to develop a golf course maintenance mission statement consistent with your perception of the vision of the club. In either situation, you should strive to obtain ownership by your staff in the mission either through involvement in its development or through orientation and training, by coaching, and by setting an example.

Goal Setting

Key Points
- Goals define manageable steps to mission accomplishment.
- Goals work because they:
  - focus attention and action
  - mobilize energy and effort
  - increase persistence
  - encourage development of good work habits
- Effective goals are *Specific, Measurable, Attainable* but challenging, *Rewarding* and *Timed* (SMART)

Ownership of the mission by everyone is crucial to attaining the vision. Goals consistent with the mission serve to direct effort and enhance efficiency by defining manageable steps toward the mission. Goal setting is used by the superintendent to enable the golf course maintenance staff to maximize their contribution to the mission of the club.

Goal setting is a proven planning tool. Research shows overwhelming evidence that managers and employees who set goals are consistently more productive. Locke and Latham (1984), in reviewing available research studies, found an 11–27% increase in productivity when goal setting was used compared when goals were not set.

Why Goals Improve Performance

The effectiveness of goals in improving performance is explained by a basic theory of human behavior; that behavior is affected by antecedents and consequences. An antecedent is an event that prompts or triggers a certain action or behavior. The ringing of a telephone is an antecedent that prompts the behavior of picking up the phone. Once the behavior occurs, some consequence results. In the case of the telephone, we find out who is calling. Dry weather (the antecedent) can prompt us to increase irrigation (the behavior), with the consequence of improved fairways.

In goal setting, goals are the antecedents. By setting a goal, the superintendent initiates behavior or actions necessary to achieve the goal. The desire to achieve the goal is often based on the anticipation of positive consequences. For example, a goal of maintaining a tournament-condition course could result in improved fertilization, effective pest control, and well-adjusted machinery. These are all behaviors required to achieve the consequence—a tournament-condition course.

Let us analyze why goals increase performance by examining a goal of having a tournament-condition course by a specified date. This goal focuses attention on green speed, fairway conditions, etc., that are necessary for the course to be in tournament condition. The goal also focuses energy and effort toward what is needed to attain and then keep the course in tournament condition. Without the goal, productivity could lag as staff members get tired or bored; the goal increases persistence by providing an incentive during these periods of lethargy. Since accomplishment of the tournament condition course is difficult, the golf course maintenance staff is more likely to be innovative and committed to improving their skills and work habits.

Characteristics of Effective Goals

To be most effective, goals should have specified characteristics. These characteristics or attributes are easy to remember by thinking of the letters in the word SMART. The letters stand for *Specific, Measurable, Attainable, Rewarding,* and *Timed. Specific* and *Measurable* goals direct action more effectively than vague or general goals. A goal of improving the training of maintenance staff employees is neither specific nor measurable. A goal of improving employee knowledge of pesticide application is quite specific, but not very measurable or quantifiable. A goal of five employees acquiring pesticide certification is both specific and measurable.

The level of difficulty is also critical to the effectiveness of goals. If goals are sufficiently challenging but still *Attainable*, energy and effort are mobilized and better job performance results. However, unrealistic goals actually can lead to lower commitment and performance. A goal of restoring a severely damaged green to tournament condition in one week is unrealistic and could cause those involved to lose motivation because they see no hope of reaching the goal. On the other hand, a goal that is too easy can become a performance ceiling, inhibiting further improvement.

People enjoy a sense of closure when a goal is accomplished, yet often feel uncomfortable when a job is unfinished. These feelings fuel persistence toward goals. Willingness to exert effort over extended periods of time wanes unless the attainment of the goal is *Rewarding*. Rewards for goal achievement can vary by employee and include increased pay, praise, recognition, or just a sense of accomplishment and pride.

Established goals encourage employees to develop the tactics necessary to reach the target by leading employees to the essential activities of tactical planning and mapping out a course of action. This process, which is the topic of the next section, is expedited by the presence of a target date; consequently, goals need to be *Timed*.

Tactical Plans

Key Points
- Tactical plans help the manager actualize goals.
- Written tactical plans are more likely to be implemented.
- Effective meetings are well-managed.

The last piece in the vision, mission, goals, and tactics pyramid presented in Figure 2.1 is tactics, which are the specific actions to be taken. Tactics are best contained in tactical plans designed to ensure that goals are accomplished. Tactical planning answers the question "What action is to be taken?" Tactical plans are used to translate decisions into actions. They map activities to be accomplished in order to meet goals.

Tactical plans answer the following questions:

- What task is to be done?
- Who is responsible?

- Where is the task to be done?
- How is the task to be done?
- When is the task to be accomplished?

Writing out tactical plans helps the manager clearly define the tasks to be done to accomplish goals. Writing down the plan ensures its completeness and increases the likelihood of its successful implementation.

A sample tactical plan addressing the goal of eliminating potential pesticide and nutrient errors is presented in Figure 2.2. The focus of the tactical plan is to train employees in correct pesticide and nutrient procedures. Note the detail of the plan and utilize a similar format for your tactical plans.

Your Responsibilities as a Planner

No matter how urgent the labor tasks become, your management responsibilities are more important. One advantage of excellent planning is that the time requirement for management can be minimized during busy periods; its importance, however, is never diminished. Below are hints to help you focus on planning.

1. A daily planning tool should be used to ensure that all tasks are delegated or completed. The tool can range from a simple TO DO list to a sophisticated planner, depending on your needs and preferences.
2. Well-planned and effectively managed staff meetings are important to maintaining focus on the mission, refining and implementing tactical plans, and maintaining communication among the staff.
3. A brief daily get-together, perhaps over refreshment, can solidify the daily plan and handle any unusual situations.
4. Resist the temptation to stop writing out tactical plans because the tactics are obvious or are only a list of deadlines.
5. Constantly reinforce the mission of the golf course maintenance operation to maintain and increase ownership of the mission.

One of the reasons labor seems more urgent than management is because there is a routine to labor and an expectancy of its completion. You can maintain your management intensity by giving it a routine and an expectancy by setting aside specific times for management.

Figure 2.2. Example of a Tactical Plan. Goal to be actualized: Eliminate Potential Pesticide and Nutrient Errors

What task or activity is to be done?	Who is responsible?	How and/or where should the task be done?	When to perform task or activity (deadline, frequency, under what conditions)
Identify training needs of staff	Golf Course Superintendent (GCS)	Meet with each staff member as possible	Complete by Sunday, July 5
Contact consultant to determine availability	GCS	Phone	Today or tomorrow
Schedule training	GCS	Check staff schedules and consultant meeting place	By Friday, July 3, or early next week
Alter schedule so all can attend	GCS		By Sunday, July 5
Meet with consultant to plan training	GCS		Before training
Hold training	GCS consultant	Local restaurant and golf course	By July 8
Meet to discuss follow-up questions	GCS	Office and on course	One week after training

The time you set aside for management has two components. The first is a continuing evaluation of the success of your plan. This need not be formally completed every day, but should have an established time and frequency. You should be continuously conducting this informal evaluation even as you perform your labor activities. This often is referred to as management by "walking around." The second component is the daily planning previously discussed.

A final comment concerns the importance of timing. Golf is a seasonal sport, especially in northern climates. As the season winds down, the golf course superintendent should shift more attention to planning. The first order of business is to discuss the vision and review the mission statement and goals. This year's accomplishments can then be reviewed and tactical plans developed for next season.

Summary

We often have heard the saying, "The best laid plans of mice and men oft go astray." It is your responsibility as the golf course superintendent to see that the vision and mission set for your golf course are achieved. In order to effectively manage golf course staff and ensure a successful future for your course, you should engage in goal setting and strategic planning.

The planning process begins by establishing a vision and a mission for the golf course together with other members of the organization. Focus on where the club hopes to be in the future, and what you hope to have accomplished. Then formulate a mission statement that embodies that vision. Once the mission statement has been created, you must gain commitment to that mission from all employees of the organization.

Setting goals consistent with the mission statement will direct staff toward achievement of the golf course mission. The goals set should be SMART: *Specific, Measurable, Attainable, Rewarding,* and *Timed.*

Once these goals are set, tactical plans, or the action steps necessary to achieve goals, are then made. A written tactical plan is extremely effective for mapping out the action steps to be taken, by whom, and when. Leading and managing the golf course staff is your most important responsibility, but by taking the time to effectively plan for the golf course staff, you can reduce the time requirement needed for management and have more time for the technical aspects of your job.

References

Covey, S.R., A.R. Merrill, and R.R. Merrill. 1994. First things first: To live, to love, to learn, to leave a legacy. Simon & Schuster, New York.

Hutt, G.K., E.A. Claypoole, J.B. Kauffman, III, and R.A. Milligan. 1989. A management resource notebook. Ithaca, New York: Cornell University, A.E. Ext. 89-22, September.

Locke, E.A. and G.P. Latham. 1984. Goal setting: A management technique that works! Prentice-Hall, Inc., Englewood Cliffs, NJ.

Mali, P. 1965. Managing by objectives. Pitman Publishing, New York.

Milligan, R.A. and G.K. Hutt. 1989. A conceptual and operational framework for teaching management to farm managers. Ithaca, New York: Cornell University, A.E. Staff Paper No. 89-27, August.

3

Organizational Structure

Employees want to know what their job is and what performance is expected. Uncertainty about job expectations is a common cause of employee dissatisfaction. A well-defined organizational structure forms the basis for employee-supervisor relationships that provide clear expectations and feedback. Organizational structure relates to the formal supervisory relationships in the golf course, not its financial or legal structure. In a golf club with an effective organizational structure, each employee knows who his/her supervisor is and each employee knows and respects the integrity of the structure. This chapter focuses on developing and implementing an organizational structure that provides a framework in which the human resource management practices can be most effectively utilized to meet the vision and mission of the golf course.

Organizational structure impacts the golf course superintendent at two levels. First, the superintendent is a part of the leadership of the golf club. The effectiveness of relationships with the golf pro, committee chairs, owners, club manager, and others is influenced by this structure. Second, the superintendent is the architect of the organizational structure of the golf course maintenance staff. The principles and ideas in this chapter apply to both levels. The discussion first focuses on the leadership structure. The maintenance staff structure is addressed in the latter part of the chapter.

As your career progresses or your golf course expands, your position as golf course superintendent is likely to have increasing management responsibilities with less time spent working on the course. Although this logical progression usually results in greater compensation and reputation, it does not always result in increased job satisfaction. The decrease in job satisfaction often comes from the move away from the technical aspects of golf course maintenance.

As golf course superintendents define the organizational structure of the golf course maintenance staff, they can define their own role to prevent this decrease in job satisfaction. First, they should retain responsibility for carrying out one or more of their favorite maintenance tasks. In addition, retaining several maintenance tasks ensures that the superintendent will maintain close contact with the maintenance staff.

More important, the superintendent must establish relationships with middle managers (assistant superintendents) and employees that keep the superintendent closely involved in the maintenance of the golf course. The emphasis of this involvement should be in using your management and technical expertise to help middle managers and employees develop plans and solve problems. By clarifying job responsibilities and developing a team orientation, golf course superintendents can succeed in their responsibilities as a manager while maintaining their interest in golf course maintenance.

Golf Club Leadership Team

Key Points
- Developing a clear leadership structure is difficult, but essential.
- The leadership team establishes strategy and policy.

Golf course superintendents, like all managers who are responsible for one part of a larger organization, want a clear understanding of their roles and responsibilities. They need to understand their responsibility and account-ability to the owner, green committee, board of directors, or general manager. Additionally, they need to understand what responsibility and authority they have and do not have for golf course maintenance. Clarity of these roles and responsibilities helps to ensure job performance and job satisfaction.

Developing a leadership structure for the golf club that provides this clarity is not straightforward; in fact, it is difficult. Golf clubs and courses have organizational challenges much like other organizations. Proprietary courses are similar to other small businesses, with family involvement often a key component. Clubs and municipal courses have organizational issues similar to other nonprofit organizations.

It is easy to conclude that family and membership involvement is in conflict with a clear, straightforward organizational structure; however, the apparent conflict can be resolved. To understand how to approach this dilemma, ask the following two questions:

- Does the Chief Executive Officer (CEO) of a corporation have complete authority?
- To whom does the CEO report?

The answers, of course, are that the CEO does not have complete authority; in fact, the CEO is hired to implement the strategies and policies adopted by the corporation's board of directors.

This same approach can be used by a golf club to involve committee members in strategic decisionmaking and policy setting, and by a proprietary course to involve family members. Members of a formal board of directors of a corporation each have input into strategic and major policy decisions. Similarly, the leaders of your club or course are those who formulate strategic direction and make major policy decisions. To determine who has this decisionmaking power—that is, who makes up your leadership team—try answering the following question: Who would be integral to making a decision to add nine holes to the golf course?

The best way to better understand this "leadership team" concept is to consider who would constitute this group at your golf course. Obviously, the leadership team varies depending upon the type of course. Consider the following examples:

Private Club: The officers of the club, the committee members, and the managers (for example, the golf course superintendent, golf professional, and/or club manager).

Municipal Course: Political officials responsible for the course, members of any elected or appointed committees, and the managers.

Proprietary Course: The owners, involved family members of owners, any advisory committees or boards, and the managers.

The success of your golf club or course is greatly influenced by the effectiveness of this leadership team. The team, which includes you as the golf course superintendent, has responsibility for establishing the vision and mission for the course and for making major strategic and policy decisions. A crucial role of the team is to establish the organizational structure for the course, including the roles, responsibilities, levels of authority, and accountability of the management positions, including the golf course superintendent.

Finally, and perhaps most difficult, the members of the leadership team must refrain from exceeding their authority by becoming involved in day-to-day operations. It is no more appropriate for a "leadership team" member other than the superintendent to become involved in daily course maintenance than it is for a General Motors board member to intercede in assembly line operation.

In the case of a private club, actual implementation of these roles is particularly difficult because committee members play golf, bringing them directly in contact with golf course maintenance staff; in contrast, the General Motors board member has no reason to be on the assembly line. This challenge increases the need for a planned organizational structure where every member of the "leadership team" clearly understands his or her role. Members, other than the golf course superintendent, must understand that when they are on the course, they should observe but never intercede. They should use their observations in future "leadership team" discussions or report them directly to the superintendent.

The Golf Course Superintendent

The golf course superintendent has the dual role of serving as a member of the leadership team and as the member responsible to the leadership team for golf course maintenance. In this dual role, the superintendent must participate in establishing vision/mission and strategic decisionmaking, represent and potentially involve maintenance staff in leadership team deliberations, and gain maintenance staff commitment to the vision/mission and strategic decisions of the leadership team.

The superintendent's position in the leadership team is shown in Figure 3.1. Two possible links between the superintendent and golf course leadership are diagrammed. The first organizational diagram (Figure 3.1a) is very common; the golf course superintendent, the golf professional, and the club manager report directly to the leadership team. The second structure (Figure 3.1b), with a general manager, is often found at large clubs. In this structure, the general manager provides the direct link to the leadership team and has overall responsibility for the implementation of the course strategies and policies.

Golf Course Maintenance Staff

Key Points
- Types of organizational structure include centralized, decentralized, mixed, and integrated team matrix.
- Each employee should have one supervisor.
- Responsibility and authority must be balanced.

Figure 3.1

The Leadership Team Organizational Structure

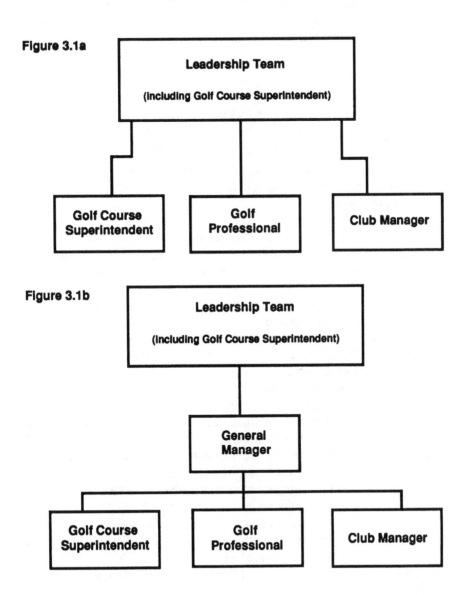

Figure 3.1a

Figure 3.1b

The golf course superintendent has the responsibility of establishing the organizational structure of the golf course maintenance staff. A clear, effective organizational structure can contribute to the following:

- Each person is aware of the vision, mission, and goals for the course.
- Each person is committed to achieving the course's goals. Often this means playing an active role in developing the goals and planning how they can be achieved.
- Each person is thoroughly familiar with and understands the roles of other staff members.
- The organizational structure includes a plan for people to work in a climate conducive to open communication and problem solving.
- Lines of responsibility, authority, and accountability are clearly established and understood by all employees.
- An atmosphere of "team effort" prevails, and each staff member is committed to the task at hand, as well as to understanding and appreciating others.

These conditions can be encouraged by any of four types of organizational structures for the maintenance staff: centralized with a broad span of control at the top; decentralized and tall; mixed; and integrated team (Kilmann, 1984). The first structure (Figure 3.2a), centralized management, is prevalent in small organizations. Power and authority are retained at the top of the organization; this structure would require almost all decisions to be made or approved by the golf course superintendent. Supervisors in this type of organization often believe they are extremely vital to the daily operation of their course and that day-to-day operations would not stay intact long without them onsite (Jackson, et al., 1986).

Decentralized structure is characterized by an increase in the authority and responsibility of middle management such as assistant golf course superintendents (Figure 3.2b). Decisions in this type of organization are frequently made by those close to where the alternatives selected are implemented (Kotter, et al., 1986). In this structure, the golf course superintendent focuses more on managing and developing managers, with the assistant superintendent and other staff supervising the maintenance tasks.

A third structure is mixed (Figure 3.2c), and displays elements from both centralized and decentralized. Often, an organizational structure evolves slowly, rather than as one planned change (Molnar, 1979). This mixed configuration can be observed at golf courses during rapid expansion or transition.

A fourth structure is the integrated team matrix (Figure 3.2d). In this configuration, participative management is pervasive and employee commitment is potentially very high. This structure succeeds only with an empowered and motivated staff. A highly decentralized structure should be

Figure 3.2

Diagrammatic Representation of Organizational Structures

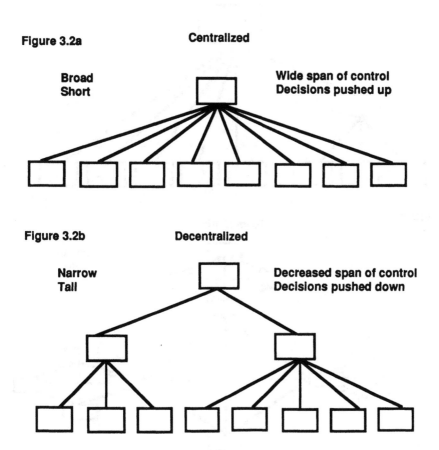

Figure 3.2a   **Centralized**

Broad   **Wide span of control**
Short   **Decisions pushed up**

Figure 3.2b   **Decentralized**

Narrow   **Decreased span of control**
Tall   **Decisions pushed down**

an intermediate step to this structure. Self-directed work teams are a common form of this structure.

The type of structure employed on a golf course is a function of management philosophy, the abilities of personnel, and the size of the organization (Killen, 1977). The truly astute golf course superintendent uses the advantages and disadvantages of each structure, and rationally and consciously chooses which organizational form to use (Killen, 1977). The three issues discussed below—unity of command; responsibility and authority; and delegation—are critical to the selection and implementation of an organizational structure.

Figure 3.2 continued

Figure 3.2c

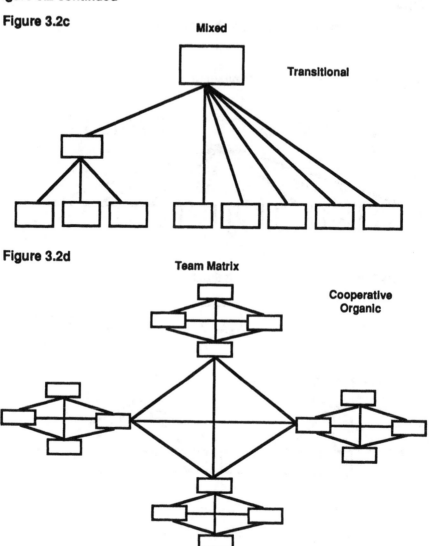

Figure 3.2d

Unity of Command

The basis of unity of command is that each maintenance staff employee should have only one supervisor (Figure 3.3), and the employee must know who their supervisor is. That supervisor should be responsible for establishing goals for employee performance, developing accountability for those

Figure 3.3

**Correct and incorrect chain of command structure for one
and two levels of management**

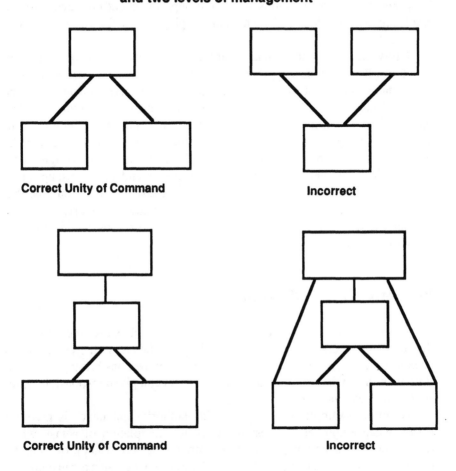

Correct Unity of Command   **Incorrect**

Correct Unity of Command   **Incorrect**

goals, providing feedback on performance, and listening to employee concerns. The employee should receive directions only from the supervisor or from someone clearly identified by the supervisor.

Even in a centralized structure where the superintendent supervises all maintenance employees, unity of command problems can occur. Examples include the golf pro demanding a maintenance employee's assistance, and the green committee chair directing an employee. Let's consider the golf pro example in more detail. Even if the pro's request is cleared by the superintendent, the maintenance employee can be placed in a situation of competing directions, unless the superintendent informs the employee prior to the pro's demand for assistance. When this situation or any similar situation is correctly handled, the employee knows whose directions to follow at all times. This situation can be handled by the superintendent instructing the employee to follow the pro's directions or by the superintendent conveying to the employee the conditions under which the employee must follow the directions of the pro.

Unity of command problems are more common in a decentralized structure where the assistant golf course superintendent supervises some or all maintenance staff employees. It is very easy for the superintendent to become a second supervisor as diagrammed in the bottom right of Figure 3.3. The inherent lack of clarity can also provide the opportunity for an employee to appeal to a second "supervisor" when dissatisfied with the outcome with the first supervisor. Correct unity of command is maintained by clear agreement between the superintendent and the assistant superintendent concerning supervisory responsibilities. An example division of responsibility could be that the superintendent is responsible for personnel matters of hours, vacations, evaluations, etc., while the assistant superintendent is responsible for training and assignment of tasks.

Responsibility and Authority

When employees are held responsible for tasks, they also must be given the authority necessary to successfully complete the tasks. If an employee's responsibility is greater than the authority granted, responsibility will shrink. If more authority is granted than is needed to meet a given responsibility, responsibility expands.

A simple example of a responsibility/authority imbalance is giving a maintenance employee the responsibility for completion of a task while rigidly specifying the time required to complete the task or not providing the necessary authority to complete the task. The employee's success in completing the task is then dependent on the superintendent's ability, not the employee's, to predict the time and other resources needed to complete the responsibility.

Delegation

Effective delegation can provide the responsibility and authority necessary for a person to successfully complete an assignment. Effective delegation requires that:

1. The expected outcomes should be clearly specified. The outcomes should be stated as SMART (*Specific; Measurable; Attainable,* but challenging; *Rewarding; Timed*) goals discussed in the previous chapter.
2. The available resources are clearly specified. The financial, decisionmaking, material, and personnel resources must be delineated.
3. The accountability for results must be clearly specified. When accountability is limited only to the final goals, the superintendent has no way to monitor progress without appearing to usurp delegated authority. Approval of plans and specified progress reports are examples of good accountability mechanisms. Often the first goal is to provide a plan for discussion and review by a specified date in the near future.

Summary

In golf course management, organizational structure is sometimes viewed as unwanted and unnecessary bureaucracy. This view originates from an emphasis on managing greens and fairways while ignoring human resources—a perspective which is very narrow and limiting.

A far more powerful view is to consider people as the most important resource of the golf course. With this view, developing a structure that helps accomplish established objectives becomes most important. As a golf course superintendent you have the unique role of being both a member of the organizational leadership structure and creator of that structure.

The first component of organizational structure to develop is the leadership team, consisting of individuals at the course who have a role in key decisionmaking, including yourself. This team is integral to successful golf course management and should be carefully considered. The team is responsible for establishing the organizational structure of the golf club or course. The organizational structure should be developed integrating elements of centralized, decentralized, mixed, and integrated teamwork matrix structures. Also, when developing an organizational structure, the leadership team must consider the elements of unity of command, responsibility and authority of individuals, and delegation.

Development of the organizational structure for the maintenance staff is the second component of organizational structure. Although this may seem simple since you have total responsibility, the same elements must be continued. One challenge to keep in mind is to protect the maintenance staff from unity of command violations emanating from elsewhere in the club structure.

The development of an organizational structure defines clear supervisor-subordinate relationships, clarifies performance expectations for employees, and creates open channels for communicating the organization's vision, mission, and goals for success.

References

Jackson, J., C. Morgan, and J. Paolillo. 1986. Organization theory: A macro perspective for management. Prentice Hall, Englewood Cliffs, NJ.

Killen, K. 1977. Management: A middle management approach. Houghton Mifflin, Boston, MA.

Kilmann, R. 1984. Beyond the quick fix: Managing five tracks to organizational success. Jossey-Bass, San Francisco, CA.

Kotter, J., L. Schlesinger, and V. Sathe. 1986. Organization text, cases, and readings on the management of organizational design and change. Richard D. Irwin, Homewood, IL.

Molnar, J. 1979. A framework for the conceptual analysis of farm organizations. Presented at the Annual Meeting of the Rural Sociological Society. Burlington, VT.

4

Controlling to Ensure
Goal Achievement

We complete our framework for the effective management of personnel by considering the question "What must we do to ensure that we meet the goals established in planning?" This requires that we consider the controlling function of management to introduce a procedure for monitoring progress toward goal achievement.

Key Points
- Controlling means ensuring that events occur according to the plan and result in goal achievement.
- Controlling focuses on the present.
- Controlling focuses on monitoring performance and making adjustments as needed.

Controlling is important because a manager's job is to achieve goals. The golf course superintendent is responsible for providing a course that meets or exceeds the golfers' expectations. The purpose of controlling is to ensure that current events conform to plans. It involves a continual monitoring of daily outcomes.

Controls can be very simple. Asking someone who is repairing a piece of equipment to call at noon and report on progress places a measurable control point on the project. Another simple example of control is crossing items off a TO DO list. This enables you to monitor and control your progress toward the goal of completing the items on the list. Control systems also can be much more formal and involved. As with planning, the effort put into control systems should be appropriate to the size of the organization and the tasks being controlled.

The most common controlling mistake is the *lack* of a control system; without a control system, events and activities proceed unchecked. Often no control exists because no measurable standard is associated with a goal. Control standards are required to measure the progress toward the goal. For example, the golf course personnel could have a goal that 90 percent of the members evaluate the course positively at the end of the season. In this example, golfers could be surveyed during the season to check on progress toward the positive evaluation goal.

The goals established in developing tactical plans (Chapter 2) are the starting point in the four-step control process:

Step 1.   Establish control standards based on established goals.
Step 2.   Develop a control plan.
Step 3.   Monitor and report the performance data.
Step 4.   Evaluate performance against control standards and interpret the need for corrective action.

The process is initiated by completing the first two steps, and the final two steps are carried out at intervals prescribed in the plan. We have provided an example of each control step in the box following the discussion of each step. The example is a green speed goal.

Control Step 1—Establish Control Standards Based on Established Goals

The goals established in planning and included in the tactical plans are the starting points for establishing control standards. These goals are often too outcome-oriented to use as control standards. Control standards must provide a status report on progress toward meeting the goal. As a simple example, you could have a goal of completing all the activities on your TO DO list by the end of the day. Since you will not know whether that goal is accomplished until the end of the day, you could set a control standard that half the activities be completed by noon.

A second example could be a goal to control golf course maintenance costs to the same level as the previous year. The goal relates to total annual costs, and thus is not known until the end of the year. A control standard must be established that will measure the status of progress toward this goal. A possible control standard would be that the year's expenses to date be no greater than the comparable year-to-date total from the year before. This could be monitored each month.

In the previous example, the goal concerning total cost involved a parameter that must be broken down into its components to develop usable control plans. The components are referred to as control points and the level of the control point is referred to as the control standard.

Example—Establish Control Standards

The personnel at the Successful Valley Country Club have established a goal that the putting green speed be consistent and greater than 10 feet for all holes for their annual tournament.

Because they intensify their maintenance program the final two weeks before the tournament, their control standards are slightly less stringent prior to the two-week period. In this case the control standard is the same as the goal, namely speed of putting green as measured by a Stimpmeter. The control standards are:

- Prior to two weeks before tournament:
  - Course average of at least 10 feet.
  - No hole less than 9 feet, 6 inches.
- Last two weeks before the tournament:
  - All holes at least 10 feet, 3 inches.
- Change in green speed:
  - Never exceed 3-inch decrease in a week.

Control Step 2—Develop a Control Plan

The control standards serve as the basis of the control plan. The control plan must identify:

- What information must be collected.
- How the information is to be collected.
- How often the collected information is to be compared with the control standard.
- Who is responsible for seeing that the control plan is implemented.

The control plan must detect problems quickly and efficiently. The control plan, therefore, needs to be a current and continuous process. To ensure success, data must be collected for all control standards. A properly designed and executed control system helps ensure goal achievement.

In operation, the control plan should pinpoint quickly where corrective action is needed. This principle is accomplished by highlighting deviations from control standards. In the cost control example, the bookkeeper or accountant should prepare a concise monthly report for the golf course superintendent to monitor progress toward the goal of no increase in total expenses. This report should highlight costs for the current period and the year-to-date compared to the control standards derived from the preceding year's costs. A complete accounting of the month's expenses would lose this control information in a sea of details.

Control is best handled closest to the source of action. Deviations detected by the control plan (plus or minus) should be immediately available to the person in a position to make a correction. If workers are to direct and control performance, they must know what is happening. Making progress reports available to those who are doing the work creates a climate where employees can adjust their own performance, as opposed to being told. The golf course superintendent can function as a coach, providing feedback and support rather than acting as a judge and policeman. The control process focuses on controlling **results,** not controlling people.

Example—Develop Control Plans

The control plan in Figure 4.1 defines the time interval for green speed measurement and the corrective action for each control standard established in Step 1, if performance is below the standard. The information collected is the information identified in the introduction to Step 2.

Control Step 3—Monitor and Report Performance Data

The actual measuring, collecting, recording, and reporting of data can proceed as detailed in the control plan. Reports give the golf course maintenance staff feedback on a day-to-day basis or over longer periods of time, as

Figure 4.1 Control Plan for Controlling Green Speed

Input or Output to Monitor	Monitoring Procedure (including who)	Monitoring Time Interval	Control Standards	Corrective Actions to Bring System Back into Control
Speed of putting green	Measure during maintenance; report to superintendent	M W F until two weeks before tournament	>9 feet 6 inches and course average > 10 feet	See green maintenance plan
Speed of putting green	Measure during maintenance; report to superintendent	Every day the last two weeks before tournament	All holes > 10 feet 3 inches	See green maintenance plan
Change in speed of putting green	Calculation compared to previous week	M W F	Weekly decrease not to exceed 3 inches on any hole	See green maintenance plan

defined by the control plan. Reports may be in the form of a chart or as simple as a verbal message on the phone reporting the status of a machine being fixed. The key is that the information must be timely, and directly comparable to the control standards. The reports should make it easy to pinpoint quickly where deviations are occurring. The priority in reporting methods should be simplicity and timeliness. Detailed accounting reports received at the end of the year or several weeks after the end of the month might impress an accountant but would have little value in meeting the no-increase cost control goal.

Example—Monitor and Report

Each Monday, Wednesday, and Friday, the golf course superintendent receives information on putting green speed from those maintaining the greens. The average green speed for all the holes and the change from the previous week are then calculated and compared to the control standards. In the last two weeks prior to the tournament, this step occurs every day.

Control Step 4—Evaluation and Interpretation

The purpose of control is to quickly detect when current performance may not lead to goal accomplishment. Evaluating and interpreting the information generated by the control plan is where this purpose is realized. Actual performance is first compared to the control standards to determine if there are any unacceptable deviations. This comparison is then used to decide whether corrective action is required. This decision involves asking the question, "Will the goal be achieved?" If performance is not meeting control standards, but goal achievement is still likely, changing the plan may be unnecessary or even detrimental.

When performance meets or exceeds the control standards, the usual interpretation is that the plan is working and leading to successful goal achievement. The astute golf course superintendent still carefully interprets the situation just in case uncontrollable factors, like weather, are causing performance to exceed control standards while hiding defects in the tactical plan. In the green speed example, just barely meeting the control standard during excellent weather could lead to a conclusion that goal achievement is problematic in poorer weather.

The more common time to consider corrective action is when performance fails to meet the control standard. In that situation, the inclination is to alter the plan immediately. First, however, you should ask the question, "Is the plan still working?" The answer could still be "yes" under the following conditions:

- The performance failure is caused by an unexpected development in uncontrollable variables, like weather.
- Performance is not responding as quickly as expected, but progress has started and the goal is still attainable.
- Contingency plans already are in place and have been or are being implemented.
- The plan is producing the best possible results, meaning the goal was not achievable.

Corrective action should only be taken when improved performance will result. When corrective action is needed, the golf course superintendent must reevaluate the plan. Generally, corrective action involves revising the tactical plan, sometimes with revised goals. In severe situations, the reformulation could involve selecting a different solution, introducing a new solution or even defining a new problem. After the corrective action is formulated, the control plan should also be reconsidered.

It is crucial that the control plan and its implementation be focused on locating and correcting deviations from the plan. When control is focused on performance to achieve the goals, it creates a sense of accomplishment and team spirit. However, reduced motivation and deteriorating morale usually occur when individuals feel that they are being blamed for not achieving desired results.

Example—Evaluation and Interpretation

Whenever a deviation is detected or whenever the same hole is consistently close to deviating from the control standard, the superintendent personally inspects the hole and reviews the maintenance plan in light of recent weather patterns before deciding whether further action is needed.

Summary

This discussion of control completes the discussion of the management framework. The establishment of the golf course vision and mission establish direction and enable commitment. The organizational structure provides a framework for personnel to effectively interact. The control plan provides a mechanism to determine goal achievement. The remainder of this book focuses on the people skills in staffing and directing necessary to work with this management framework to maximize productivity and employee satisfaction and development.

References

Hutt, G.K., E.A. Claypoole, J.B. Kauffman, III, and R.A. Milligan. 1989. A management resource notebook. Ithaca, New York: Cornell University, A.E. Ext. 89-22, September.

Jerome, W.T. 1961. Executive control—the catalyst. John Wiley & Sons, New York.

McGregor, D. 1967. The professional manager. McGraw-Hill, New York.

Scanlan, B. 1974. Management 18: A short course for managers. John Wiley & Sons, New York.

5

Employee Recruitment: Attracting Qualified Applicants

Attracting a qualified workforce is one of the greatest human resource concerns of small business managers. Golf course superintendents are no exception. In a small organization, recruitment becomes more critical because each individual is such an important part of the workforce.

The job of recruiting and selecting new employees is a top priority. Most employers can remember an instance when the "right person" was hired and the result was outstanding performance and a high level of job satisfaction. Conversely, when the "wrong person" is hired, the result can be poor performance, costly mistakes, and low morale for the entire staff.

Cohn and Lindberg (1984) emphasize the importance of recruitment and selection over other personnel functions in their book, *Practical Personnel Policies for Small Businesses,* with the following recommendation:

> Spend about ten times more time and money hiring people than training them. That is a practical thought for the smaller firm where all assets are usually in short supply, especially the most valuable—the time of its key people. That time should be devoted to selecting the best people, not to training or bolstering those who are selection errors.

A mistake in hiring is only magnified the longer the person is on the job. In this chapter we look at the issue of attracting qualified applicants to golf course positions. We start by looking at the external environment—factors that affect a manager's ability to attract good workers. Planning to recruit is then addressed, followed by a discussion of recruitment methods with special emphasis on employment advertising.

45

The External Environment

Key Points
- External factors often affect the recruiting process.
- External factors include economic conditions, demographics, immigration trends, and labor regulations.

In the recruitment process, a golf course superintendent or any employer must deal with two environments. The first is the organization's internal environment, over which the superintendent has a great deal of influence. In the case of human resource management, internal issues include how employees are recruited, paid, trained, etc. The second—the external environment—is one that the superintendent must always be aware of, but may not be able to substantially influence. For example, a nearby factory may create strong competition for qualified workers by paying high wages. By being aware of how various external factors affect the recruitment of qualified employees, an employer can adjust internal recruiting strategies accordingly.

The most important external factors currently facing golf course superintendents include economic conditions, demographics, immigration trends, and labor regulations. At times employers see these issues as barriers to effective management. However, using them as an excuse for a poor recruitment process is counterproductive. Understanding these external factors and developing effective recruiting tactics allows an employer to increase the chances of successfully hiring the best people. Let's look at how each of these external factors relates to the process of recruiting and hiring qualified employees.

Economic Conditions

Economic conditions have a substantial impact on the labor market. During periods of slow economic growth, unemployment rates are likely to rise, causing a surplus of available workers. During these periods it may be relatively easy to draw a large pool of highly qualified candidates. Conversely, when the economy is booming, unemployment rates drop and there is more competition for highly qualified workers. As economic conditions push wages up, all employers are pressured to pay higher wages.

Demographics

Demography is the study dealing with the human population, its distribution, and vital statistics. Demographic factors are continually affecting employment. In the past, typical golf course workers were young white males between the ages of 16 and 25. In recent years, however, the makeup of the golf course staff and the workforce in general has changed because of shifts in the general population. As the baby boomers enter middle age, there is a much smaller pool of workers between the ages of 16 and 25. As a result, employers have drawn on non-traditional pools of workers, including retirees, immigrants, and women. Changing demographics will continue to force employers to tap labor pools that traditionally they have not used.

Immigration Trends

Over the past half century, immigrants have increasingly provided more of the manual labor for U.S. business and industry. Immigrants who are willing to work long hours in low-skill or manual-labor jobs continue to play an important role in the U.S. labor market. Workers from a variety of ethnic backgrounds (particularly Asian and Latino) are increasing dramatically and, as a result, these groups will represent a higher percentage of the workforce. This trend will require that managers improve their skills in working with a culturally diverse staff. The number of immigrant workers in golf course maintenance positions is increasing. This change puts more pressure on superintendents who employ immigrants to understand new cultures and to overcome the language barriers that divide English-speaking and non-English-speaking workers.

Local Labor Market Conditions

Each geographic area has its own set of unique labor conditions which affect golf course employment. Some areas may have several large companies that provide strong competition for labor. Conversely, an economically depressed area may have an abundance of entry level workers. The local labor market conditions affect the local labor supply and consequently impact human resource efforts, including recruitment, training, and compensation.

Labor Regulations

Both federal and state governments continue to enact a variety of laws to address various workforce issues. These laws include benefit programs such as unemployment insurance and workers' compensation, safety regulations, minimum wage legislation, and others. When new laws are enacted, compliance often requires more recordkeeping and sometimes more expense for the employer. However, laws exist to protect the employer and the employee and in most cases are consistent with good human resource management practices.

Identifying Personnel Needs

Key Points
- Planning is essential to recruit effectively.
- Recruitment planning requires assessing the situation, developing a job description, and taking the time to recruit properly.

The first step in recruiting applicants for a golf course maintenance position is determining staffing needs. Each time a position opens up there is an opportunity to upgrade the staff and hire people with more of the skills needed to maintain the course. A vacancy should be viewed as an opportunity to fill the position with someone who is even more qualified or skilled than the person who left. Proper planning will increase the chances of hiring people who can make the greatest contribution. There are several steps in the planning process.

Assess Your Situation

Each manager has his or her own personal style of supervising, which should be considered through self-assessment as part of the staffing process. For example, a manager who is a very authoritative leader might consider selecting a candidate who works well under close supervision. On the other hand, someone who is an empowering leader may be inclined to hire an individual who is self-motivated and likes to work with a minimum of supervision. Taking time to think about your management style and the qualifications for the position you are trying to fill will improve the chances of finding the "right" person.

Develop a Job Description

Developing a new or updated job description for the vacant position is an important part of the planning process. A job description is a general listing of the qualifications and the skills needed for a given job. It documents the type and range of responsibilities required. Using a job description in the recruiting process has two important advantages. First, it forces the supervisor to clarify the responsibilities in writing; this process forces the supervisor to make critical decisions regarding how the position will be defined. Second, the job description is a communication tool that allows the employer to convey the same information to each applicant during the selection process. Used this way, it can prevent future misunderstanding about job requirements and provide a basis for discussion as the position evolves.

Some employers have resisted using job descriptions for fear that an employee will refuse to do a task, saying, "It's not in my job description." A job description is not cast in stone; it can be changed as the requirements of the job change. Most important, it communicates the primary aspects of the job to the person who will perform it.

All employees on the golf course staff should have job descriptions. Preparing job descriptions is useful, since defining and updating positions will make the responsibilities of the job clear to both the manager and the employee. When the job description is developed or updated, it is important to review and discuss it with the employee to encourage involvement and goal commitment.

The key elements of a job description generally include:

1. Job Title
2. Position summary, including who supervises the position
3. Typical duties
4. Knowledge, skills, and abilities

Figure 5.1 provides an example of a job description for the position of Assistant Golf Course Superintendent.

Make Time To Recruit

Perhaps the most common mistake golf course superintendents make in recruiting potential employees is not investing the time and effort required to

Figure 5.1:

Sample Position Description
Successful Valley Country Club

Title: Assistant Golf Course Superintendent

Position Summary: Under the direction of the Golf Course Superintendent, to instruct and supervise staff in golf course maintenance operations, including mowing, fertilizing, and pest control.

Typical duties include supervision of:

- Mowing and trimming greens and tees.
- Bunker maintenance, including edging, weeding, and raking.
- Loading, unloading, and handling golf course maintenance materials, including fertilizer chemical containers, soil, sand, and mulch.
- Fertilizing, spraying, and verticutting golf course turf.
- Daily course setup of hole location and tee marker placements.

Knowledge, Skills, and Abilities:

- Ability to train and supervise employees.
- Ability to operate, troubleshoot, and perform routine maintenance on assigned mowers.
- Knowledge of fertilizer and pesticide application rates and procedures.
- Ability to adjust and operate mowers to ensure precision mowing of tees and greens.
- Willingness to continually learn and improve golf course maintenance practices.
- Ability to lift at least 100 lbs and to perform heavy manual labor at times.

---

do the job well. Since golf courses typically operate seven days a week, a vacancy in one position can create major problems if there is not a plan to replace an individual who resigns suddenly or is sick for an extended period of time.

Having contingency plans for backup labor during the golfing season is a critical part of the recruiting process. Backup labor allows your staff to get the work done in a timely fashion and maintain golf course quality while a position is temporarily vacant.

Unfortunately, many managers make the mistake of not having sufficient temporary or backup labor to see them through difficult times. The cost of not having backup workers is high. Jobs not completely or correctly performed over the period of a day or several days can create substantial costs in the form of lower productivity, poor quality, costly mistakes, and golfer dissatisfaction. By planning for backup workers, the manager allows sufficient time for the recruiting process and increases the chances of attracting the most qualified and productive worker to fill the vacant position, instead of hiring the first person to come along. Employers can use a variety of backup strategies, including having extra part-time workers available and hiring people from a temporary agency. Also, some managers keep people on their staff who can be called in at a moment's notice to fill in when the need arises.

The Recruitment Process

Key Points
- An effective recruitment process results in a strong applicant pool.
- There are seven common recruiting methods.
- A combination of recruitment methods should be used to develop a strong applicant pool.
- Help wanted ads should be written with care.

Recruitment is the process of attracting individuals on a timely basis, in sufficient numbers, and with appropriate qualifications to apply for jobs within an organization. This definition implies an organized process, as opposed to hiring employees on a walk-in basis. Businesses often recruit many more applicants than are actually needed to fill a position. How many applicants would you need to end up with several to whom you would offer the job? Assume that a golf course attempting to fill a position ran a series of newspaper and magazine advertisements to recruit applicants. The ads generated résumés and applications from 30 applicants. Fifteen of these applicants were judged to be potentially qualified. These 15 were screened for the eight most qualified. Of the eight applicants, six chose to come for an interview. Three of the applicants were worthy of being offered the job. Only one of the three was willing to accept.

This scenario illustrates the importance of having a sufficient pool of applicants from which to choose. During good economic times, the relative number of applicants and acceptances decreases because job seekers have more alternatives. The size of the applicant pool is important because we want a pool large enough to include several well-qualified applicants. If an applicant pool includes no one who is qualified, it is advisable to start the recruiting process over until qualified applicants are found.

While we strongly encourage golf course superintendents to develop an applicant pool, we also recognize that this may not always be desirable or feasible. For example, an excellent candidate may walk in to apply for a job or a current employee may recommend a highly qualified friend. In situations like these, a larger applicant pool may not be necessary if the individual is qualified. However, it is extremely important to use the selection procedures described in Chapter 6 to determine whether the individual is capable of meeting your performance standards.

Recruitment Methods

There are many sources of job applicants. The keys are to choose the recruitment methods that will provide the best pool of applicants from the variety of those available, and to use the selected recruitment methods effectively. Let's take a look at seven common methods of attracting good employees and discuss the value of each in a recruiting program:

1. **Suggestions from current employees**—Current employees can be an excellent source of contacts for new employees. They know people in your community and they have a good idea of your labor needs. They also have a stake in the process since they are likely to be working with the person they suggest if he or she is hired. This approach, while effective and very common throughout the golf industry, should be used with care. The same criteria for hiring another applicant should be used when hiring friends or relatives of a current employee. If the new person does not succeed in the job, there could be friction between the manager and the employee who suggested the applicant. Some employers offer a cash bonus to employees who refer job applicants who are eventually hired.

2. **Word of mouth**—This technique has been very successful for many employers and is the most common recruitment method. Friends and professional contacts can refer potential candidates if they know you are looking. There are also networks of professionals (such as seed and pesticide sales representatives) who

get around to many golf courses and may be in a position to refer prospective applicants. While this is a preferred recruiting method, it may not always work; during times of tight labor supply it may not draw a sufficiently large labor pool, or it may fail to draw the most qualified applicants.

3. **Want ads**—A frequently used recruitment method is placing a want ad in local newspapers or in trade publications. This approach has several advantages: it is quick, it is relatively inexpensive, and it provides a way to reach a potentially large audience. But newspapers and magazines also have a drawback: Often superintendents complain that these ads bring them applicants, but none they would want to hire. Perhaps this problem stems from how the ad is written. If the ad specifically describes the desired qualifications, many unqualified individuals will screen themselves out naturally. Hints on how to write a want ad are covered later in this chapter.

4. **Government job services**—In the United States, almost every state has a job service program (provided by the state department of labor) with county offices that provide valuable services to employers who request them. Golf course superintendents and other employers can call the job service when they are seeking applicants for a vacant position. A counselor will help the employer define the job and write a job announcement. The announcement will then be posted in the job service office (without the name of the employer). Interested applicants go to job service personnel to request more information. Job service personnel screen the applicants and refer qualified individuals to the employer. The state job service often is under-utilized by employers, because the pool of qualified workers is sometimes limited. However, there are numerous examples of employers who have used government job services with great success. Keys to working with the local job service include making a personal contact with a local job service representative and establishing yourself as a respectable employer and clearly communicating your labor needs.

5. **College placement offices**—Placement offices at both four-year and two-year colleges can be a source of desirable applicants. Graduates seeking golf course work are in demand. By developing contacts at these colleges, the golf course superintendent is in a strong position to recruit some excellent staff members who may stay with the golf course over the long term.

6. **Posting job announcements**—Job announcements are another recruiting approach. If you have a written job description,

writing a job announcement is fairly easy. Take the key responsibilities from the job description and write an announcement to post on bulletin boards in the community. Job service counselors can also help with this process.

A job announcement should contain the following information:

- Title of job
- Description of responsibilities
- Description of skills required
- Description of working conditions, if appropriate
- Key components of the wage/benefit package, if appropriate
- How to apply

After a suitable job announcement is prepared and duplicated, post it in areas where potential employees will see it. Such places might include bulletin boards at agricultural college career offices, high schools, shopping centers, and stores. It also might pay to distribute the announcement to employees and other key contacts so they will have the details if they meet a potential applicant.

7. **Search firms**—A number of private firms (sometimes known as "headhunters") make a business out of finding prospective employees for employers with vacant positions. In the golf industry, most of these firms operate at the superintendent level and can be helpful to directors or managers of a club looking for a highly qualified superintendent or assistant superintendent. An important consideration in deciding whether or not to use this alternative is cost. Most search firms work on a commission basis and may charge the employer from 10 to 30 percent of the new employee's annual salary. However, many employers who have used these services for high-level positions have reported good results.

Employers commonly use only one or two recruiting methods. Word of mouth referrals are by far the most common. However, using only one or two recruiting methods may not generate an adequate pool of applicants. In a tight labor market, a variety of recruiting methods is recommended.

In addition, hard work and creativity will improve the effectiveness of each recruiting method. For example, some golf course superintendents use want ads to recruit job applicants, but often the ads are written hastily without sufficient thought. Many fail to "sell" the position. In today's job environment, aggressive marketing of open positions can pay off handsomely, if done carefully.

Writing a Help Wanted Ad That Sells the Position

It is not unusual to pick up a local newspaper and find an ad that reads, **"Golf course worker wanted. Call 333-4444."** To recruit the best applicants, the want ad must provide information that is important to the applicant as well as sell the position. The following steps demonstrate one way to write better help wanted ads and recruit more qualified applicants:

- Step 1. Give the appropriate job title.
- Step 2. Say something positive about the business.
- Step 3. Describe the job.
- Step 4. Highlight positive working conditions.
- Step 5. If appropriate, provide information on wages and benefits.
- Step 6. Indicate how to apply.

Using these steps, a more appropriate advertisement which sells the position might look like this:

> **Golf course maintenance position: Historic, local country club seeks individual for general golf course maintenance. Duties include mowing, trimming, raking sand traps, and other similar responsibilities. Competitive wages, 50 hours per week, overtime pay. Work with a modern line of well-maintained equipment. Opportunities for advancement. Fill out application at Successful Valley Country Club, 123 Country Club Drive, Successful Valley, PA 54321.**

This approach to advertising a golf course position has several advantages. It provides useful information, covering all elements of a job announcement, as described earlier. It enhances the position of the golf club as a place of employment. It sells the position and increases the opportunity to attract an excellent candidate from another job. Finally, because so many people look at the want ads, it may increase substantially the size of the applicant pool. Also, by requesting applications, you can build a file of potential candidates for the future, and minimize telephone interruptions from potential applicants.

Targeting Labor Pools

As indicated earlier in this chapter, external forces can affect a golf course superintendent's recruiting efforts. Demographic factors make it advisable at times to target non-traditional workers in the recruiting effort. Depending upon the positions available, a variety of labor pools may provide potential candidates. Some potential labor pools include: retirees, high school students, college students, disabled workers, and part-time workers who are moonlighting from another job. By targeting one or more specific labor pools, it is often possible to address the seasonal workforce issues that superintendents face and to improve the success of the recruiting process. For example, seasonal work demands may make it desirable to target high school and college students and retirees. Once the decision is made regarding which group to target, the next step is to decide where and how to recruit. For example, word of mouth and newspaper ads may be most effective for seasonal employees.

Summary

The purpose of the recruiting process is to attract a qualified pool of applicants for openings on the golf course maintenance staff. The process begins with clearly defining the position to be filled. The golf course superintendent increases the chances of attracting the best candidates by using a variety of recruiting methods effectively, rather than relying on just one or two methods. The seven most common recruiting methods are: (1) suggestions from current employees, (2) word of mouth, (3) want ads, (4) government job services, (5) college placement offices, (6) posting job announcements, and (7) search firms. Since external factors like the economy, demographics, immigration trends, and labor regulations affect the recruiting process, the manager must adjust the recruiting process to accommodate them. Golf course superintendents most successful at recruiting have established a reputation as good employers by providing competitive compensation, effective management, and safe, comfortable working conditions. Once an acceptable pool of applicants has been recruited, the selection process can begin.

References

Cohn, T. and R.A. Lindberg. 1984. Practical personnel policies for small business. Van Nostrand Reinhold Publishing, New York.

Heneman, H.G., D.P. Schwab, J.A. Fossum, and L.D. Dyer. 1986. Personnel/Human resource management. Third Edition. Richard D. Irwin, Homewood, IL.

Johnston, W.B. and A.H. Packer. 1987. Workforce 2000: Work and workers for the 21st century. Hudson Institute, Inc., Indianapolis, IN.

Plunkett, R.W. 1979. Supervision: The direction of people at work. William C. Brown Company, Dubuque, IA.

Shapley, A.E. 1970. Personnel management in agriculture: Instructor's manual. Rural Manpower Center. Special Paper No. 12. Michigan State University.

Thomas, K.H. and B.L. Erven. 1989. Farm personnel management. North Central Regional Extension Publication 329-1989.

6

Employee Selection:
Choosing the Right Person

Although the recruiting process and the selection process are often viewed as one continuous effort, there is an important distinction between them. The recruiting process focuses on generating a pool of candidates that includes several qualified people, and the selection process focuses on choosing the best candidate for the job. **Employee selection is the process of choosing from a group of candidates the individual or individuals who will be offered a position.** The objective is not simply to hire a person, but to hire the "right" person. It matters whom you choose. The best employee is often several times more productive than a poor employee.

The Selection Process

Key Points

There are four selection methods that aid the supervisor in predicting future performance of an applicant:

- The application provides basic information about applicants.
- The interview process can provide valuable information about a candidate if it is carefully planned and conducted.
- Checking references provides valuable information about an employee's performance in previous jobs.
- Trial periods can be the best way to judge future performance.

In the selection process, the manager tries to predict the future performance of an individual candidate and, in doing so, attempts to make the best
hiring decision. Predicting performance is a difficult task, but effective use of
the proper selection tools makes it easier. Consider a golf course superintendent who has a job vacancy and is attempting to fill it quickly. The
position is announced by word of mouth, and a candidate shows up to inquire
about the job. The superintendent decides to conduct an interview on the spot.
The superintendent asks the candidate three or four questions about previous
work experience, knowledge of golf course practices, and general qualifications for the job. The candidate then answers each question as positively as
possible, emphasizing all past experience that has anything to do with land-
scaping or golf course management. After the interview the superintendent
decides to hire this first applicant.

No doubt, many employees have been hired this way, particularly when
a superintendent is short-staffed. However, when we look at the effectiveness
of the previously described interview and hiring process, serious limitations
are apparent. The interview described is not organized; a random set of
questions is used. Most candidates try to show all their qualifications in the
most positive light, and sometimes embellish or exaggerate their qualifications
in hopes that they can land the job and then learn what they need to know
after they are hired. An unorganized interview is, at best, a meager selection
tool for predicting performance. In fact, the interview process itself has
limitations as a predictor of performance, even though it is almost always
used. It is best to use the interview process in a systematic, planned way and
to augment that process by using other selection tools as well. Other selection
tools include application forms, reference checks, and trial periods. A
combination of these tools used effectively can substantially increase the
chances of hiring the right person and ultimately enhance the performance of
the golf course staff. All are discussed in this chapter.

The Application

Information provided on the application concerning previous education,
job experience, and length of service can be a good predictor of future
performance (Heneman 1986). The application form should be concise,
gathering only the information needed to make effective hiring decisions. In
many cases, the golf course or country club will have a standard application
form used by all employees. This form should request the information
necessary to effectively screen job candidates. In some cases, however, it
may be advisable to develop an application that specifically meets your needs.
An application form should focus on previous education and on previous job
experience.

Used effectively, job application forms offer a number of advantages. Applications can reduce time spent in the recruiting process by eliminating the need for someone on the golf course staff to talk to each applicant. Office personnel can be trained to accept applications as candidates drop in to inquire about jobs. If the application requests the correct type and depth of information, a group of applications can be screened in a relatively short period of time, allowing the supervisor to spend more time with qualified applicants. Applications of qualified candidates can also be kept on file for an extended period of time, so that they are available during the next round of recruiting.

The Interview Process

The interview is the most common selection tool managers use. From a practical standpoint, it is appropriate for the supervisor to meet a job applicant, ask that applicant questions and provide the applicant with an opportunity to make comments and ask questions. The interview process is still important and recommended; however, instead of an informal discussion with the job applicant, an interview should be a structured discussion between the employer and the job applicant focusing on job-related issues and predicting future performance.

The following suggestions help structure the interview process and improve its usefulness as a predictor of future employee performance:

Step 1: Prepare for the interview

Before conducting the interview, determine the personal and performance characteristics that you will be looking for in the interview process. Based on those characteristics, develop a written list of questions that you will ask each applicant. Interview preparation has four parts.

- **Part 1:** Determine a small number of applicant characteristics about which you want to gather information. Characteristics such as job knowledge, mechanical skills, interpersonal skills, and work habits should be evaluated in interviews. Do not try to identify every possible characteristic that might relate to the job. Instead, choose from four to six characteristics about which you are going to gather information.
- **Part 2:** Write a list of questions that will elicit information on these characteristics. Ask open-ended questions rather than questions that require a simple yes or no answer. Include in your list several probing questions that will help you find out as much

Figure 6.1.

Sample Interview Questions

This list of questions is intended to provide ideas for developing your own list of interview questions.

1. Job-Related Questions:

What skills do you bring to a golf course maintenance job?
Can you work 7 a.m. to 3 p.m.?
What experience have you had with mower operation and maintenance?
Describe any formal education or training in horticulture.
Describe work experiences from previous jobs that would be relevant to this job.

2. Probing Questions:

What did you like most about your last job?
What did you like least about your last job?
How well did you get along with your supervisor and coworkers on your last job?
Why are you looking for a new job?

3. General Recruitment Questions:

What is your salary/pay requirement?
When would you be available to start?
Do you have any questions for me (us)?

---

as possible about the applicant. Figure 6.1 provides a sample list of interview questions.

- **Part 3:** Plan to ask each applicant the same questions in the same sequence. This step is critical to ensure reliability in the interview process. That is, it increases the chances that the "right" candidate will be chosen. Only by requesting the same information from each applicant will an interviewer be able to fairly compare applicants.
- **Part 4:** Develop a rating system to score each performance characteristic you are interested in (Gatewood and Field, 1987). A scoring system is extremely helpful when you attempt to summarize and interpret a large volume of information. For

example, if you develop a 1 to 5 scoring system and score the answer to each question, you will have a quantitative way to compare candidates after each has been interviewed.

This 4-step process helps to formalize the interview and make it a more reliable predictor of employee performance. This process—used in combination with the other selection methods—will increase the chances of selecting the right person.

Step 2: Put the applicant at ease

It is natural for a job applicant to be nervous at an interview. Obviously, the more formal the interview, the more relevant this issue. It is important to make the applicant feel as comfortable as possible. The more you do to alleviate tension, the more meaningful the interview will be. A handshake and a friendly smile are good ways to start. Make it a priority to find a quiet, comfortable place where the interview may be conducted without interruption.

Step 3: Listen

Open the discussion, but encourage the applicant to do most of the talking. An interviewer who dominates the conversation or answers questions for the applicant will learn very little about the prospective employee. Use open-ended questions that require an explanation rather than a "yes" or "no" response. By using this technique, the interviewer is likely to get the candidate to open up and provide more valuable information. Make a note of any follow-up questions you want to ask later in the interview.

Step 4: Resist personal bias

Keep impressions and personal opinions to yourself during the interview. An applicant who gets a sense of your values or feelings on certain topics may tailor responses to fit those values or feelings. Do not overlook qualified applicants because of their religion, ethnic background, age, sex, or disabilities. Bias and discrimination are discussed in detail later in this chapter.

Step 5: Fulfill your responsibilities to the applicant

Remember that the applicant also has a stake in finding out something about you and the job. Based on the information you provide, an applicant must decide whether to accept the job if offered. The applicant will want to know as specifically as possible what your management style is and what it is like to work at your golf course. Be honest, but at the same time sell the strengths of the position. Give the applicant plenty of opportunity to ask questions.

Provide the applicant with a written outline of the wages and benefits that employees receive. Put as much information as possible in writing so the applicant knows exactly what to expect and can refer to the information later.

Leave adequate time to introduce the applicant to other employees. If appropriate, give the applicant a brief tour and be sure to describe any unfamiliar equipment or facilities. Be sure to "sell" the positive aspects of employment at your golf course.

Step 6: Notify applicants of their status

Finally, let applicants know when a final decision will be made. As soon as applicants have been eliminated as candidates, let them know. It is not fair to keep them waiting if they are no longer being considered for the job.

Checking References

Personnel executives responsible for hiring hundreds of employees each year put high priority on reference checks in conjunction with the interview process. Consistently checking references is an important hiring practice for any organization regardless of size.

While references can be checked at any time, it is usually more practical and less time-consuming to narrow down the top candidates for the job before starting to check references. Ask the applicants to provide several references. The more information you have, the better equipped you are to make a decision.

The following are examples of some questions you may want to ask a previous employer:

1. How long did you employ the individual?
2. What was the person's quality of work?
3. How much responsibility was the worker given?
4. How did the individual get along with fellow workers?
5. Was it necessary to provide close supervision?
6. Why did this worker leave?
7. Would you rehire the individual?

Again, a rating scale of 1 to 5 may be used to measure each response and allow you to summarize the responses at the end of the reference-checking process.

In these days of lawsuits and potential liability, some past employers may refuse to provide information on previous employees. That is their right. Nevertheless, you should make every effort to get a sampling of the references to ensure that you are able to make an informed choice.

Trial Periods

Employers want to avoid making selection mistakes that will result in poor performance or other employment difficulties. One effective way to accomplish this objective is to hire new employees on a trial basis. A trial period may last from 30 to 90 days. To introduce a trial period, let the applicant know how long the trial period is and indicate that at the end of the period, you and the employee will make a mutual decision regarding whether to continue employment. While employers still must comply with the payroll and legal requirements, a trial period provides the superintendent with the opportunity to observe individual job performance. Is the new employee good with equipment? Can the trial worker follow directions? Does he or she show up regularly and on time? Use this opportunity to observe the person's interpersonal skills. How well does this individual get along with supervisors and other staff members? Compared to the other four predictors of performance discussed, trial periods potentially can be the best predictor of future performance because you have an opportunity to observe work being performed.

Avoiding Personal Bias

Key Points
- The five common biases are: stereotyping, the halo effect, first impressions, projection, and contrast.
- The manager should be aware of the common biases and resist being influenced by them in the selection process.

As indicated, one way to make the interview a more reliable predictor of performance is to use a standardized approach. Likewise, it is important to avoid letting your personal biases enter into the selection process. Bias can lead you to interpret applicant information incorrectly and can result in a hiring error. By recognizing the most common personal biases, the interviewer is in a better position to resist letting bias unduly influence the hiring decision (Douglas, Klein, and Hunt, 1985). The most common selection biases include:

1) **Stereotyping** is the tendency to attribute certain characteristics to particular groups of people. For example, you might think that the work ethic of an immigrant worker is much better than the work ethic of local workers and have a tendency to hire immigrant workers for that reason. This bias could influence your thinking and prevent you from selecting a local worker with an excellent work ethic.

2) The **Halo Effect** is the tendency to regard highly an individual who has a personal or work characteristic that you particularly like. The halo effect might cause an interviewer to disregard some negative qualities of an applicant. Assume, for example, that an applicant shows up for a job interview well-groomed and neatly dressed. The halo error tendency would be to assume that the person is competent in a number of job areas for which you are recruiting simply because personal appearance created a favorable impression.

3) A **First Impression** is the tendency to distort or ignore additional information about an individual to fit your first impression. The first impression an interviewer receives of a job applicant can greatly influence the entire assessment of that person. For example, if an applicant impresses the interviewer in the first few minutes of the interview, the remainder of the interview is positively influenced. The converse can be true as well. If the first impression is poor, then the remainder of the interview can be negatively influenced. In each case, there is a chance to be so influenced by the first impression that the primary purpose of predicting future performance becomes a secondary issue.

4) **Projection** is the tendency to attribute one's own motives, feelings, or values to others. For example, an interviewer who is neat and organized tends to assume that an applicant is the same way. This type of projection might be right, but it is just as likely that it is wrong, and an error would impair the hiring decision.

5) **Contrast** is the tendency to measure an individual against someone with whom we have just had contact. If a manager has just interviewed a substandard applicant, a mediocre applicant may look great by comparison. In this case, contrast bias may lead to hiring a mediocre candidate instead of waiting to find one with outstanding qualifications.

Discrimination

> **Key Points**
> - Discrimination in employee selection and other aspects of employment is illegal.
> - State and federal laws prohibit discrimination based on age, sex, marital status, race, color, creed, religion, national origin, disability, or physical handicap.

No discussion of selection practices would be complete without addressing issues of discrimination as defined by current state and federal laws. Discrimination and bias are two closely related issues. In fact, discrimination is likely to stem from stereotyping and projection biases. Employers in general are becoming more aware of the legal difficulties that may arise from personnel problems. Increasingly, employees are likely to take legal action if they feel that they are being unfairly treated. Remember, discrimination can be committed by any member of the golf course staff. While it is beyond the scope of this book to discuss all the subtleties regarding labor law and discrimination, golf course superintendents and their supervisors should be aware of the primary areas of discrimination law and how these laws affect applicant recruitment, selection, and hiring, as well as other aspects of employment.

Title VII of the Civil Rights Act of 1964 provides the basis of federal anti-discrimination law. Later amended by the Equal Employment Opportunity Act of 1972, it covers organizations employing 15 or more people. Together these two pieces of legislation create the foundation for discrimination law in the United States. In addition to these federal regulations, many states have established their own employment discrimination laws. Sometimes state laws are stricter than the federal ones, and typically, if state and federal laws cover the same issue, the stricter law takes precedence. It is the responsibility of the golf course superintendent, supervisors, and other management level employees at the golf course or club to be aware of and comply with both state and federal laws relating to employment.

The purpose of this discussion of discrimination is to acquaint the reader with basic discrimination issues. Basically, employers are prohibited by federal and state law from discriminating against employees or job applicants on the basis of:

- age
- sex or marital status

- race, color, or creed
- religion or national origin
- disability or physical handicap

The following discussion of discrimination law is from *The Employee Rights Handbook,* copyright 1991 by Steven Mitchell Sack. It has been reprinted with permission of Facts On File, Inc., New York.

Sex Discrimination

The law requires similar employment policies, standards, and practices for males and females. Equal treatment applies in a variety of areas, including hiring, placement, job promotion, working conditions, wages and benefits, layoffs, and discharge.

The following checklist will familiarize you with the kinds of practices that are illegal. In general, it is discriminatory for an employer to:

- Refuse to hire women with preschool-age children while hiring men with young children.
- Require females to resign from jobs upon marriage when there is no similar requirement for males.
- Include spouses of male employees in benefit plans while denying the same benefits to spouses of female employees.
- Restrict certain jobs to men without offering a reasonable opportunity for women to demonstrate their ability to perform the same job adequately.
- Refuse to hire, train, assign, or promote pregnant or married women, or women of childbearing age merely on the basis of sex.
- Deny unemployment benefits, seniority, or layoff credit to pregnant women, or deny a leave of absence for pregnancy, irrespective of whether it is granted for illness.
- Institute compulsory retirement plans with lower retirement ages for women than for men.

Age Discrimination

Federal and state discrimination laws are designed to promote employment of older persons based upon their abilities, irrespective of age. They also seek to prohibit arbitrary discrimination and to help employers and workers find ways of addressing problems arising from the impact of age upon employment. Age discrimination law protects workers who are over age 40 and under age 70.

The following thumbnail sketch outlines what employers *can* do under federal and state discrimination laws pertaining to age:

- Fire older workers for inadequate job performance and good cause (e.g., tardiness or intoxication).
- Entice older workers into early retirement by offering additional benefits (e.g., bigger pensions, extended health insurance, substantial bonuses, etc.) which are voluntarily accepted.
- Lay off older workers, provided younger employees are similarly treated.
- Discriminate against older applicants when successful job performance absolutely requires that a younger person be hired for the job (e.g., in the case of a flight controller).

However, the following actions are *prohibited* by law:

- Denying an older applicant a job on the basis of age.
- Imposing compulsory retirement before age 70.
- Coercing older employees into retirement by threatening them with termination, loss of benefits, etc.
- Firing older persons because of age.
- Denying promotions, transfers, or assignments because of age.
- Penalizing older employees with reduced privileges, employment opportunities, or compensation because of age.

Racial Discrimination

The law generally forbids private employers, labor unions, state and local government agencies, and employment agencies from:

- Denying an applicant a job on the basis of race or color.
- Denying promotions, transfers, or assignments on the basis of race or color.
- Penalizing workers with reduced privileges, reduced employment opportunities, and reduced compensation on the basis of race or color.
- Firing a worker on the basis of race or color.

Recognize that discrimination can occur during any number of the following employment stages: recruiting, interviewing and hiring, promotion, training, transfer and assignment, discipline, layoffs, and discharge procedures.

Religious Discrimination

The Civil Rights Act of 1964 prohibits religious discrimination and requires employers to reasonably accommodate the religious practices of employees and prospective employees. This law covers employers of 15 or more persons. Various state laws also prohibit discrimination on the basis of creed—for example, due to a person's observance of a certain day as a Sabbath or holy day. In New York, for example, employers may not require attendance at work on such a day except in emergencies or in situations in which the employee's presence is indispensable. Absences for these observations must be made up at some mutually agreeable time, or can be charged against accumulated leave time.

- Employers have an obligation to make reasonable accommodations to the religious needs of employees and prospective employees.
- Employers must give time off for the Sabbath or holy day except in an emergency.
- In such an event, the employer may give the leave without pay, may require equivalent time to be made up, or may allow the employee to charge the time against any other leave with pay except sick pay.

However, be aware that:

- Employers may *not* be required to give time off to employees who work in key health and safety occupations, or any employee whose presence is critical to the company on any given day.
- Employers are *not* required to take steps inconsistent with a valid seniority system to accommodate an employee's religious practices.
- Employers are *not* required to incur overtime costs to replace an employee who will not work on Saturday.
- Employers have *no* responsibility to appease fellow employees who complain they are suffering undue hardship when a co-worker is allowed not to work on a Saturday Sabbath due to religious belief while they are required to do so.

- Employers are *not* required to choose the option the employee prefers, as long as the accommodation offered is reasonable.
- Penalizing an employee for missing a workday because of refusing to work on Christmas or Good Friday most likely constitutes religious discrimination, depending on the facts.

Disability Discrimination

Until recently, the main federal law protecting handicapped individuals against discrimination was the Rehabilitation Act of 1973, which applied to government contractors and employers who receive federal assistance. This law prohibits denying an otherwise qualified applicant or employee a job or opportunity, including fringe benefits, promotion opportunities, and special training, solely on the basis of a handicap. Further, employers who have government contracts or subcontracts worth over $2,500 must take affirmative steps to employ and promote handicapped workers and must not discriminate against them.

Due to the limited applicability of the Rehabilitation Act of 1973, on July 26, 1990, Congress enacted the Americans With Disabilities Act (ADA) [P.L. 101-336]. The Equal Employment Opportunity Commission has jurisdiction and enforcement authority over Title I of the ADA, prohibiting employment discrimination against anyone with a disability.

The law protects any person with a physical or mental impairment that substantially limits "one or more major life activities." This covers a broad range of disabilities, including deafness, heart disease, cancer, AIDS, and emotional problems; it even covers alcohol or drug abusers who rehabilitate themselves. Ever since the law took effect (in July 1992 for employers with 25 or more workers, and in July 1994 for employers with 15 or more workers), companies have been bound to:

- Eliminate any inquiries on medical examinations or forms designed to identify an applicant's disability.
- Avoid adverse classifications of job applicants or employees because of disabilities.
- Avoid participating in a contractual relationship, including a collective bargaining agreement, that has the effect of discriminating against job applicants or employees with disabilities.
- Avoid discriminating against an applicant or employee because of that individual's relationship or association with another who has a disability.

- Make reasonable accommodations to the known physical or mental limitations of an applicant or employee, unless doing so would impose an undue hardship on the employer.
- Avoid denying employment opportunities to an applicant or employee if the denial is because of the need to make reasonable accommodation to a disability.
- Avoid employment tests or selection criteria that have a disparate impact on individuals with disabilities unless the test or criteria is shown to be job-related and supported by business necessity.
- Administer employment tests in the manner most likely to accurately reflect the job-related skills of an applicant or an employee who is disabled.

From *The Employee Rights Handbook.* Copyright 1991 by Steven Mitchell Sack. Reprinted with permission of Facts On File, Inc., New York.

Discrimination is a serious issue that you must face as a golf course superintendent. Remember that discrimination can take place anywhere in the employment process, and a discriminatory act can be performed by anyone in the organization's staff, from the top manager down to the front desk receptionist. Discrimination issues should be discussed with your staff, especially those who are involved in the recruitment, selection, and training functions of your golf course. Information on your organization's anti-discrimination policy should be included in your employee handbook, if one exists.

This section on discrimination is intended to provide golf course superintendents with an overview of the primary issues related to employment discrimination. The reader should be aware that this section is not intended to include all of the subtleties of the law. Many state laws are different, and it is advisable to consult an attorney in areas where you have questions. The information presented here was current at the time of printing, and it is the responsibility of the golf course superintendent and supervisors to stay current with changes in the law.

Summary

The primary objective of the selection process is to choose the right person for the job by attempting to predict future performance. We have outlined four selection methods and discussed their strengths and limitations as predictors of performance. They include applications, interviews, reference checks, and trial periods. By using a combination of selection methods effectively, the chances of hiring the right person increase dramatically.

The selection process can be greatly impaired by the introduction of personal bias or discriminatory practices. If personal bias in the form of stereotyping, halo effect, first impression, projection, or contrast enters the selection process, it is less likely that the right person will be hired for the job. Discriminatory selection practices are even more serious, since legal problems can result.

By carefully utilizing selection procedures and avoiding age, sex, or other types of discrimination, employers increase their chances of hiring the most qualified and productive candidate for the job.

References

Cohn, T. and R.A. Lindberg. 1984. Practical personnel policies for small business. Van Nostrand Reinhold Publishing, New York.

Douglas, J., S. Klein, and D. Hunt. 1985. The strategic managing of human resources. John Wiley & Sons, New York.

Gatewood, R.D. and H.S. Field. 1987. A personnel selection program for small business. Journal of small business management, October 1987: 16–24.

Heneman, H.G., D.P. Schwab, J.A. Fossum, and L.D. Dyer. 1986. Personnel/Human resource management, 3rd ed. Richard D. Irwin, Inc., Homewood, IL.

Plunkett, R.W. 1979. Supervision: The direction of people at work. William C. Brown Company, Dubuque, IA.

Sacks, S.M. 1991. The employee rights handbook. Facts on File, Inc., New York.

Thomas, K.H. and B.L. Erven. 1989. Farm personnel management. North Central Regional Extension Publication 329.

7

Training for Success

Employee training is so important that U.S. employers annually spend almost as much for training as all the nation's public and private colleges and universities combined spend on education (Heneman, 1986). Golf course employees don't bring with them all the knowledge, skills, and abilities they need to do the job now and in the future, so training represents an investment in future performance, productivity, and overall golf course success.

Training is a planned process of learning experiences intended to maximize the employees' contribution to the organization. A variety of terms are associated with employee training, including growth and development, orientation, and on-the-job training. Each of these terms has a slightly different meaning, and each will be discussed in this chapter. The above definition assumes that training is performed based on a plan with predetermined goals. This point is emphasized throughout the chapter.

The Importance of Training

Key Points
- A planned training program avoids error and poor performance.
- The person doing the training must be qualified.

Failure to prepare employees for work through a planned training effort leaves their job knowledge and skill development to chance. Failure to have a training plan does not mean that the employee will not learn what to do; it means the employer will have less control over what is learned. Waste, accidents, damage to equipment, distraction of other employees, poor work quality, and inadequate performance are potential problems associated with improper or inadequate training.

A common training mistake is turning new employees loose with no training whatsoever. Once on the job, most employees without training will somehow figure out a way to get the job done as well as they can. They may figure it out themselves, or they may have other employees, equally as naïve about correct procedures, give them suggestions and tell them how to do it. Undoubtedly, this approach will result in many mistakes, some of which may be extremely costly. Without effective training it is unlikely that golf course staff members will develop to their potential. Examples include:

- Consider the employee who applied herbicide to a green at the rate of 20 oz per 1000 ft^2 instead of the recommended 5 oz per 1000 ft^2 and seriously burned a green to the extent that it would not recover for six to eight weeks.
- Consider the employee who, when instructed to check the oil on the fairway mower routinely, failed to do it over an extended period of time and ruined the engine, which cost $1,000 to repair.

Another common mistake is sending the employee to be trained by another employee who is not prepared to do an effective training job. This assumes that the employee trainer knows exactly what must be done and how to do it correctly, and has a training plan for peak performance with the least amount of mistakes. Research on training in the logging industry revealed that the informal, on-the-job method of training was by far the most common way that newer and younger employees learned the business of logging. Further, it was found that over time, as there were fewer career loggers with a lifetime of skill and experience to share with new employees, the informal on-the-job training became less effective. Trainees were unable to acquire the depth of skill and knowledge that they needed to conduct their responsibilities safely and effectively (Garland, 1979). The absence of some type of plan for training can lead to undesirable results and poor job performance.

How People Learn

Key Points
- Adult learning is a complex process.
- By understanding how adults learn, a supervisor can become a more effective trainer.

For decades psychologists have been studying human behavior and how people learn. Learning theory suggests that ten conditions must be met in order for learning to be effective:

1. **The individual must be motivated to learn.** Learners should be aware that their present level of knowledge or skill, or the existing attitude or behavior, needs to be improved if they are to perform well. Therefore, they must have a clear picture of the behavior to be adopted.

2. **Standards of performance should be set for the learner.** Learners must have clearly defined targets and standards that they find acceptable and can use to judge their own progress.

3. **The learner should have guidance.** Learners need a sense of direction, as well as feedback on how they are doing. A self-motivated individual may provide much of this personally, but the trainer still should be available to encourage and help when necessary.

4. **The learner must gain satisfaction from learning.** Learners are capable of learning under the most difficult circumstances if it satisfies one or more of their needs. Conversely, the best training programs can fail if they are not seen as useful by the trainee.

5. **Learning is an active, not a passive process.** Learners need to be actively involved with the trainer, other trainees, and the subject matter of the training program.

6. **Appropriate techniques should be used.** Trainers have a large repertoire of training tools and materials. They must use these with good judgment in accordance with the needs of the job, the individual, and the group.

7. **Learning methods should be varied.** The use of a variety of techniques, as long as they are equally appropriate, helps learning by maintaining the trainee's interest.

8. **Time must be allowed to absorb the learning.** Learning requires time to assimilate, test, and accept. This time should be provided in the training program. Too many trainers try to squeeze too much into their program and allow insufficient scope for practice and familiarization.

9. **The learner must receive reinforcement of correct behavior.** Learners usually need to know quickly that they are doing well. In a prolonged training program, intermediate steps are required in which learning can be reinforced.

10. **Trainer and trainees need to recognize that there are different levels of learning.** At the simplest level, learning requires direct physical responses, memorization, and basic conditioning. At a higher level, learning involves adapting existing knowledge

or skills to a new task or environment. At the next level, learning becomes a complex process. Learning at this level may include identifying principles in a range of practices or actions, integrating a series of isolated tasks, or dealing with interpersonal skills. The most complex form of learning takes place when training is concerned with the values and attitudes of people and groups. This is not only the most complex area, but it is also the most difficult and dangerous.

The previous section was reprinted from the book *Handbook of Personnel Management Practice,* by Michael Armstrong and John F. Lorentzen, copyright 1982, and it was used by permission of the publisher, Prentice Hall, a division of Simon & Schuster.

Growth and Development

Employers today are increasingly mindful of the need for planned employee growth and development. Employee growth and development evolves from a set of experiences designed to challenge employees and encourage them to fulfill their potential. These experiences may include supervisor coaching, increased responsibilities, education, and promotion. The implication is that employees will have a more valuable set of skills and knowledge when they leave your employment than when they started. Addressing employee growth and development needs has advantages for both the employer and the employee. To the employee, the development process can be a real motivator. The organization should reward increased knowledge, skill, and productivity with promotions, pay increases, and positive reinforcement. The employer's payoff from employee development comes in the form of increased productivity, increased morale, and a greater level of employee commitment.

Orientation

Key Points
- Successful training begins with orientation.
- Effective orientation requires empathy on the part of the manager.
- Planning is essential.
- Use a first day orientation checklist.

Case Study: Rick's first day

As Rick drove to his first day at his new job at the Successful Valley Golf
Club, he was excited, and at the same time a little apprehensive. At age 18,
Rick had held only one other job, a summer position at Burger World. The
idea of spending the summer outdoors instead of in a fast-food restaurant
really appealed to Rick, but he wondered what the first day of his new job
would be like.

The first day at Burger World was a disaster. They were short-staffed the
morning Rick arrived. The manager met him at the door, told him to get an
apron and help Bob at the grill. The manager assured Rick that Bob would
tell him what he needed to know to get him started, and then when things
calmed down, they would have time to talk. Somehow, he made it through the
lunch hour, working at the grill, although Bob seemed to resent having to
work with a new person who didn't really know the ropes.

After the rush hour, the manager apologized for the disorganization and
promised things would get better. He introduced Rick to a few staff members
and gave him papers to fill out to meet the payroll requirements. Even though
the manager seemed like a nice guy, the summer never did get a whole lot
better. Rick just performed his duties as well as he could.

Now, as Rick's car headed down the long, winding driveway into the
Successful Valley Club, he had to admit he was a little nervous. Questions
raced through his mind. What would the new boss be like? Would he get
along with him? Would he be able to do this new job, and would he like it as
well as he thought? What would the other people be like? Would he get
along with his coworkers? Would he be able to make some friends?

As Rick got out of his car, Jim Lewis, the golf course superintendent,
greeted him with a big smile and a handshake. Rick got the feeling that Jim
genuinely was glad to have hired him. Jim took Rick into the office to sit
down and review the things Rick would need to know to get started on the
right foot. Rick was impressed that Jim had notes in front of him so he
wouldn't forget anything. Jim reviewed all the basic things that one needs to
know on the first day of the job: where to park his car, what the hours of work
would be, where the restrooms were, where the lunch room was, where the
refrigerator that he could put his lunch in was, and so on.

Jim also gave Rick several employment forms to fill out immediately and
then others to fill out and bring back the next day. He gave Rick a copy of the
club's benefits handbook and employee policy handbook. Jim went on to
explain how the course was laid out, the size of the staff, the type of work that
the crew performs, and also the type of work that Rick would be doing. Jim
emphasized that the crew worked as a team and helped each other whenever
necessary. He took care to explain what Rick's role would be as part of the
team. Jim explained that everyone's goal was to maintain an excellent golf
course for the enjoyment of the members. Rick also was impressed that Jim
gave him an opportunity to speak and ask questions.

Jim had the rest of Rick's day planned out. After a 30-minute tour of the maintenance facilities and the course, Rick met with the mechanic to learn how to operate a hand mower and a string trimmer. He was then sent out with one of the more experienced employees to mow and trim the rough areas on several holes on the back nine. Twice that afternoon Jim checked with Rick to see how things were going and to make sure there was always someone nearby to answer Rick's questions. By the end of the day, Rick had met everyone on the golf course staff.

As he drove home, Rick felt good about the first day. He liked the people. He thought he was going to get along very well with his new boss. He felt confident that he would enjoy the job and do it well. He felt that if the next few months continued the way the first day had gone, it would be a great summer.

Most people can recall their first day on the job. Even those who have been on a job for 10 or 20 years or more are likely to have memories of that very first day. For most people, beginning a job is an emotional time, a time of change and excitement. It also is a time of apprehension. What happens on the first day and the first week of employment sets the stage for the months and years to come. The case above contrasts two very different orientation experiences. The Burger World experience was a failure because the manager did not plan for Rick's orientation or take into account the needs of his new employee. Conversely, Jim Lewis, the golf course superintendent, clearly made Rick's orientation a top priority for the day. The result was a positive start for the new employee.

In most cases, the golf course superintendent or supervisor spends time recruiting, screening, interviewing, and selecting the best individuals for the job. Orientation is the next step in that process. Performed well, the orientation continues the positive process begun in recruiting and selecting. The two most important attributes of a supervisor who is orienting a new employee are *empathy* and *planning*.

Empathy is the ability to put yourself in the other person's shoes—to consider how he or she feels. As a supervisor with many roles and responsibilities and full knowledge of the job, sometimes it is difficult to fully appreciate what a new employee is experiencing. For those who have worked at the golf course for a relatively long period of time, issues such as break time, where to eat lunch, and access to a telephone are matters of fact. To the recently hired employee, it is all new information. Supervisors who can put themselves in a new employee's place as orientation begins will be much more effective in getting the employee properly established.

An orientation, even for the most basic job, is most effective when it is planned. A plan should answer questions like "How can we make the new employee feel welcome and comfortable here? How should we familiarize the new individual with the course and the other people who work there?

What tasks will the new employee do first, and what tools and equipment will the individual need to be familiar with?" Answering these questions allows the supervisor to determine in advance what type of orientation is needed.

First Day Orientation Checklist

The following checklist represents a series of steps that can be followed to ensure that the orientation has been planned and is carried out effectively:

1. **Greet the employee and put him or her at ease.** A new employee is likely to be nervous during the first day on the job. Creating a warm and friendly atmosphere makes the individual feel comfortable, and is an important ingredient in getting the employee started correctly. The superintendent or other supervisor should also reassure the individual that he or she is confident that the new employee will do a good job, based on the information provided in the recruiting process. The supervisor should also make a special effort to introduce the new employee to current staff members.

2. **Review key information the employee needs to get started on the job.** Each new employee should know some basic things about the workplace. The supervisor should keep a checklist of those items and make sure that each new employee is informed of them on the first day. These items include things like the location of the restrooms, lunch and break hours and locations, the hours of work, and pay procedures. The supervisor should add any additional items to the list that are unique to the job and that the employee needs to know to get started.

3. **Give a basic explanation of the job and how the new employee's position relates to the other jobs on the golf course.** An introductory explanation of what the individual will be doing, his or her key responsibilities, and to whom the individual will report should be made at the beginning of the orientation process. If a job description has been written for the position, the first day is a good time to review it. This may also be a good time to introduce an organizational chart if you have one. Allow sufficient time to explain how to do the job. It is equally important to provide the information in easily understood pieces. Remember, the employee may be nervous and will be exposed to a lot of new information the first day. Give only the information necessary to get the employee started and follow up when further information can be assimilated.

4. **Teach the basic fundamentals of the first one or two tasks.** If, for example, the first task an employee is going to do is mowing, the supervisor might have the mechanic describe routine maintenance procedures and how to operate the equipment. The supervisor then may give specific instructions on where and how to mow. Later in this chapter, job instruction training will be discussed. The job instruction training steps can be used here to train an employee who has very little knowledge of the task.

5. **Follow up.** On the first day the supervisor should be available to answer any questions and to check on how things are going for the new employee. Promising this and following through on this promise is extremely important to building a good relationship with the new hire. If, for some reason, the supervisor cannot be available, the employee should know who to see about questions that arise. Continually encourage the new employee to ask questions and become an active participant in the training program.

After the initial orientation, employees should be given new tasks as they are ready to accept them, and as they are required in the daily work routine. Perhaps the most important activity is to follow up with the new employee to make any adjustments in work procedures or to provide necessary feedback. Obviously, some employees will learn faster than others. Each new hire should be treated as an individual and given the amount of feedback and supervision required to get a good start in the job.

The Training Process

The training process should flow naturally out of the orientation process and focus on longer-term development needs. In this section, we will address when to conduct training, offsite training, and job instruction training.

When to Conduct Training

Key Points
- Determine if there is a gap between current performance and desired performance (performance discrepancy).
- Determine if employee training is the most appropriate way to address the issue.

The first step a manager must take in the employee training process is to anticipate training needs. At times, an employee's failure to perform a task correctly is a motivation problem rather than a training problem. For example, hand raking sand traps might fall into this category. Employees may perform the job poorly because it is tedious rather than because they do not know how. Ask these four questions when assessing training needs (Heneman, 1986):

1. **Does a performance discrepancy exist?** A performance discrepancy is a gap between the employee's potential peak performance that a manager desires and the actual performance attained by the worker. Observing the individual perform the task and examining performance data when available can help determine whether a performance discrepancy does exist. In some cases, it will take careful observation to obtain the information necessary to answer this question.

2. **Is the performance discrepancy important?** If an observed performance discrepancy is likely to have a negative impact on the quality of the golf course or on working relationships, then it is important. A manager should ask: "Why is the performance discrepancy important, and what will happen if it is ignored?" Some performance discrepancies are minor, and some will take care of themselves in time. Examples of performance discrepancies that have a significant negative impact on the golf course include improper operation of a chainsaw, uneven application of pesticides, and improper mowing.

3. **Is employee training a potential solution?** Employee training may be a solution to a performance discrepancy if the discrepancy is caused by lack of ability rather than lack of motivation. When an individual's motivation to learn the job is the issue, it must be addressed and corrected before training can be initiated effectively. Finally, supervisors and coworkers must support the behaviors the employee will learn. Time and effort will be wasted if training is not reinforced on the job.

4. **Is employee training the preferred solution?** Cost effectiveness and practicality must be considered. Other possible solutions may include a job change or the introduction of instructional aids or direction sheets to assist the employee.

Offsite Training

Offsite training presents a legitimate alternative to training in the workplace if it is available at a reasonable cost. Many employers use community colleges or other training programs to teach employees specific skills. For example, a spray technician might take a Cooperative Extension application and safety course. This approach complements on-the-job training and enhances the employee's growth and development. Regardless of how much offsite training is available, much of the job training is usually done onsite. Even highly skilled employees who know how to perform when they join the staff need to be shown how the particular golf course operates.

Job Instruction Training

Key Points
- Job instruction training is a practical approach to on-the-job training.
- Job instruction training consists of five steps: Prepare, Tell, Show, Do, and Review.

Most golf course superintendents and their supervisory staff became managers after they had established themselves as competent in the technical areas of golf course management. However, a supervisor's technical competence does not necessarily translate into training ability. The key to effective training is to have a plan and to follow several key steps. The trainer must be patient and willing to understand and adapt to the needs of the learner. Perhaps the most straightforward and practical approach to on-the-job training for small business managers is Job Instruction Training, or J.I.T.

Job instruction training can be summed up in five steps:

- Prepare
- Tell
- Show
- Do
- Review

Job instruction training came into widespread use during World War II, when many industrial workers went to war, and their replacements had to learn new jobs quickly. The process became a quick, effective way to train American factory workers. The last four steps listed above are those typically referred to as job instruction training, and they are effective when training for a variety of tasks. In order to make the process more comprehensive, a preparation step has been added.

Employee Training Steps

Step 1. Prepare the worker and the workplace: Have materials and equipment ready and have the workplace properly arranged just as you want the workers to keep it. Put the workers at ease and get them interested in learning the job.

Step 2. Tell the learner how to do the task: Explain, illustrate, and question the employees carefully to see that they understand how to do the job. Stress the key points, and be patient. Be careful not to present more information than the employees can master.

Step 3. Show employees how the task is to be performed: After the careful explanation provided by Step 2, show the employee how to do each part of the job. Emphasize key points.

Step 4. Let the learner do the task: Have the employees tell and show you what they are doing, and have them explain the key points back to you. Provide feedback and continue the process until you are certain the workers know how to do the job.

Step 5. Review the work: After letting the employees perform the task on their own, return and review the quality of the work. Provide feedback that reinforces good work habits and helps the employees set goals for improvement. Encouragement is extremely important.

Figure 7.1 is an example of job instruction training in action. Note that some of the information in these training steps is provided in greater detail than may be required. This detail is provided to ensure that basic information in the training process is not overlooked.

Job instruction training is useful on a golf course because new employees must be trained each season. Some superintendents have written training sheets similar to the one above for all key jobs on the course. There are two advantages to this. First, a written list of instructions ensures that no crucial information is forgotten. The list can easily be changed or updated at any time. Second, it provides the same information for all key staff people who train, so all workers will receive the same kind of orientation.

Summary

Golf course superintendents should see the value of effective employee training programs in terms of job performance, employee morale, and elimination of costly mistakes on the job. But to be effective, training programs must be carefully planned, and adequate time must be set aside specifically for training to occur.

Figure 7.1

Job Instruction Training in Action: String Trimmer Example

Task to be taught: Operation of a gas-powered string trimmer.

Step 1. Prepare the worker and the workplace: Tell the employee what you are about to do. Create a relaxed environment where you will not be interrupted. Acquire and arrange materials needed: trimmer, ear protection, safety glasses, gasoline, oil, and extra trim line.

Step 2. Tell the learner how to do the task: Explain safety equipment issues, including clothing, hearing, and eye protection. Explain how to pull-start the equipment, how a choke works, how the throttle works, where the on-off switch is, and how to adjust the line.

Step 3. Show the employee how the task is to be performed: Show the employee how to put on safety equipment, turn switch to "on" position, adjust choke in preparation for starting, adjust throttle, and start engine. Demonstrate the back-and-forth movement required to use the trimmer safely and efficiently. Show how to tell when the trim line should be adjusted. Show how to turn the machine off, and how to adjust the trim line safely, with the machine turned off. Show how to check and fill gas and oil.

Step 4. Let the learner do the task: Give the weed trimmer to the employee and have the employee repeat the steps just demonstrated in Step 3. Provide a few handwritten notes or a checklist to help the employee remember each step. Coach the employee, making suggestions and answering questions, as needed.

Step 5. Review the work: After leaving the employee to perform the task independently, check back to see that the trimmer is operating properly and that the employee is using it correctly. Review the quality of work to see that trimming is done completely and at the correct height. Provide feedback that reinforces desirable work habits and helps the employee set goals for improvement. Encouragement is extremely important.

Managers should understand how people learn and should focus on each individual's motivation to learn, actively involving learners in the training process and utilizing appropriate learning methods and training tools for the individuals being trained. Properly designed, a training and development program can be a strong motivator for increased confidence, improved performance, and greater commitment to the course.

Successful training programs begin with a thorough orientation process. Think about what a new employee should know and plan how to most effectively present that information. The Job Instruction Training process provides a practical and effective way to train employees in almost any task. The person training must be qualified to train that particular skill. And be sure that adequate time is set aside for the training session.

Properly planned and conducted, employee training and development benefits the employee, the golf course members, and golf course management by improving job performance and leading to increased employee satisfaction.

References

Armstrong, M. and J.F. Lorentzen. 1982. Handbook of personnel management practice. Prentice Hall, Englewood Cliffs, NJ.

Baird, L.S., C.E. Schneier, and D. Laird (Eds.). 1985. The training and development sourcebook, 3rd ed. Human Resource Development Press, Amherst, MA.

Cadwell, C.M. 1988. New employee orientation. Crisp Publications, Los Altos, CA.

Garland, J.J. 1979. A look at logger training. Logger's Handbook, vol. xxxix, 6pp. (A series of the Pacific Logging Conference.)

Heneman, H.G., D.P. Schwab, J.A. Fossum, and L.D. Dyer. 1986. Personnel/Human resource management, 3rd ed. Richard D. Irwin, Inc., Homewood, IL.

Laird, D. and R. House. 1983. Training today's employees. Boston, MA.

Mager, R.F. and P. Pipe. 1970. Analyzing performance problems. Fearon Publishers, Belmont, CA.

Nilson, C. 1990. Training for non-trainers. AMACOM, New York.

8

Managing Employee Performance

Employees often want to know the answer to two questions: "What is my job?" and "How am I doing?" When properly conducted, a performance management process helps golf course superintendents provide employees with answers to both of these questions. **Performance management is the daily process of working toward previously established performance expectations followed by a formal performance appraisal.** The traditional performance appraisal or review is one element of this process. To many employers, performance appraisal refers to an evaluation, which is often conducted once a year and accompanies the process of giving employees raises. While periodic performance appraisal interviews are important, they are only a part of an effective performance appraisal system. To have the greatest impact, performance management must be a process with several phases. It should be looked at as a process of communicating performance-related information between employer and employee. Blanchard and Johnson, authors of *The One Minute Manager,* tell us "Management is something you do **with** your people, not **to** your people." A continuous constructive interchange of information is essential for the process to work effectively.

The Performance Management Process

Key Points
The performance management process has three primary steps:
    Step 1: Establish performance expectations.
    Step 2: Provide regular coaching and feedback regarding employee performance.
    Step 3: Conduct the performance appraisal interview.
The mission and goals of the course provide the focus in this process.

For performance management to work effectively, direction must come from the golf course superintendent and the supervisory staff. An effectively led organization has a clear and established direction, which comes from a formal mission statement supported by written goals, as discussed in Chapter 2. These must be considered when employee performance expectations are established. When all employees work toward the organization's mission and goals, maximum workforce efficiency and productivity can be achieved.

Figure 8.1 illustrates that the first step in the performance management process—identifying performance expectations—is tied to the mission and goals of the golf course. The integration of business goals with performance expectations is a key to improved employee performance and satisfaction. After performance expectations have been identified and communicated to the employee, the supervisor must follow up with the proper coaching and feedback to provide encouragement and to ensure that the job is performed properly. The final step in the process is a performance appraisal interview, which is usually conducted annually.

Formal and Informal Approaches to Performance Management

Not all golf course superintendents have adopted formal, written performance management procedures. Yet most superintendents evaluate employee performance to some extent. As supervisors mature in their management skills and as the size of staff increases, supervisors tend to replace informal management practices with more formal ones (Hornsby and Kuratko, 1990). Figure 8.2 contrasts informal performance management approaches with formal approaches. The long-term goal of most golf course superintendents should be to adopt practices on the formal side of the continuum, assuming that the size of the staff and the organizational structure warrant this shift.

Mission and Goals

Integrating the mission and goals of golf course management into the performance expectations of individual employees is critical in the performance management process. Employees will be more highly motivated if they understand how their performance expectations and their work contributions relate to the success of the golf course. Generally, all golf course staff members want it to succeed; they want to be part of a winning team. The

Figure 8.1.

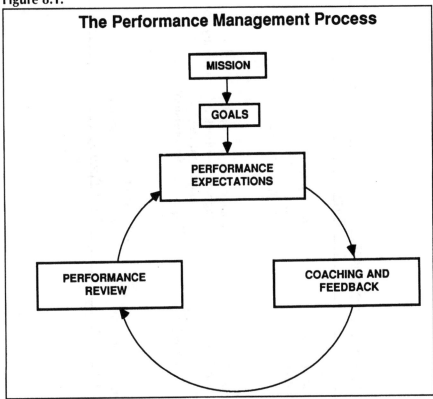

The Performance Management Process

superintendent's challenge, then, is to create a winning mission and actualize it through clear goals. Once goals are set, the performance expectations of each golf course staff member should be tied to them.

Writing a mission statement and goals is not enough to create a successful organization. The mission must be internalized by the superintendent and then communicated to the entire golf course staff. The mission can, and should, be presented in a variety of ways, including written statements given to employees. Many superintendents include the mission statement in their policy handbook or post the mission and goal statements on the employee bulletin board. Discussion of the business mission should take place in staff meetings and in each step of the performance management process. In addition, personal success should be linked to organizational success. For example, part of articulating the vision of the golf course is conveying that "when the golf course does well we all benefit." These benefits can come in the form of increased job satisfaction, better compensation, promotion, and individual recognition.

Figure 8.2. Formal vs. Informal Approaches to Performance Management

	Informal	Formal
Step 1 Performance Expectations	Verbally communicated Partially thought out Somewhat clear	In writing Well thought out Clearly conveyed
Step 2 Coaching and Feedback	Sporadic Process Feedback not complete Expectations not consistently met	Day-to-day process Ongoing feedback is both positive and negative Expectations consistently met
Step 3 Performance appraisal	No formal review Little development emphasis Low employee involvement	Formal review Development-oriented High employee involvement

Establishing Performance Expectations

At least once each year, performance expectations should be conveyed to the employee in a clear and understandable way. Individual performance expectations or standards are defined as the conditions or results of satisfactory work. They should be discussed with the employee and agreed upon before the performance period begins. Performance expectations for the individual should be consistent with the mission and goals previously discussed. When creating performance expectations, managers should consider the tasks performed in the employee's position and the employee's past performance in conducting those tasks. Performance expectations should be clear and behavior-based. That is, the employee must understand the behavior or performance required to meet established expectations. In many businesses, performance expectations are given to the employee verbally through discussions and meetings. Others believe performance expectations should be in writing and kept up to date.

Written performance expectations have several advantages. They allow the manager and employee to discuss and agree on expected performance. They also provide a permanent record that can be referred to at any time throughout the performance period. To be most effective, the establishment of performance expectations should be a two-way process where the employee has input in decisions on performance expectations. These should be based on the golf course goals and the requirements of the individual job.

Three essential components of effective performance expectations are:

1. **Measurability**—Truly result-oriented performance expectations must contain measures by which performance can be judged. Measures may include dollars, percentages, numbers of items, and ranges. By integrating measures into performance expectations, both manager and employee know clearly what level of performance is expected.
2. **Time frame**—Productivity often is determined by how quickly desired results can be achieved. The employee and the manager should be clear on exactly when results are expected.
3. **Attainability**—Performance expectations must be within the individual's and the organization's reach if they are to be an effective performance management tool. If either internal or external business constraints prevent attainability, they may demotivate—rather than motivate—the individual.

It was mentioned earlier that performance expectations should be in writing. This can be done through a frequently updated job description, if it is specific enough. A job description for the purpose of establishing performance expectations might include a general goal statement or an umbrella statement of several sentences describing the objectives of the position. The remainder of the description could include 5 to 10 specific key statements identifying the results expected in the position.

Another way to establish more specific performance expectations is through a written set of job requirements, which we refer to as a job performance guide. The job performance guide identifies the specific behaviors required to perform a job completely and correctly. Such a guide can be particularly helpful when there are a number of people doing the same job, such as raking traps, or mowing tees, greens, and fairways.

Figure 8.3 provides a sample job performance guide for mowing tees with a reel-type walk mower. Similar job performance guides can be developed for other golf course maintenance duties. Preparation of such information gives golf course superintendents and supervisors an opportunity to clarify jobs and goals, as well as providing an excellent communication and training tool to use with employees.

Coaching and Feedback

Ongoing performance feedback is critical for employee development, growth, and productivity, as well as golf course success. Yet this area of management can be fraught with difficulties. There are two types of feedback—positive feedback and constructive criticism. Positive feedback generally takes the form of compliments, recognition, and approval for performing well on a daily basis. Constructive criticism may be viewed by the employee at times as negative feedback, but in reality it provides for corrections in job behavior at or near the time the employee is doing the job. Both of these types of feedback should be provided on an ongoing basis and in a positive way.

Before we look at proper coaching and feedback skills, let's look at some reasons why managers do not always provide positive feedback and constructive criticism as much as they could:

Reasons why managers fail to provide positive feedback:

- Managers often use the excuse that it's not necessary: "Joe already knows he's doing a good job."
- Some managers have a difficult time expressing any feelings, positive or negative, to others. As a result, they often say nothing.

Figure 8.3. Sample Job Performance Guide

Mowing tees with reel-type walker mower
  1. Check fuel and oil in assigned utility cart.
  2. Check fuel in assigned walker mower and make sure it runs.
  3. Load walker walker into assigned utility cart.
  4. Be sure walker mower is not running, clutch is engaged and reel is shut off when loading and during transport.
  5. Remove all tee markers before mowing.
  6. Check tee surface for any rocks or debris and remove them.
  7. Unload walker mower and begin mowing in straight lines in the assigned direction.
  8. Empty baskets as often as necessary in the rough and away from the tee. Spread clippings in many different spots and not on plants or in flower beds.
  9. Make two cleanup cuts in opposite directions after mowing the straight lines. Make sure perimeter cut is neat and take care not to scalp the rough.
  10. Replace tee markers in their correct order in new locations on the tees. Direct tee markers straight toward the fairway.
  11. Check to be sure there are no clippings or debris on tee surface.
  12. Shut off reel drive mechanism, load walker mower into cart, shut off engine, engage clutch and proceed in same manner to the remaining assigned tees.
  13. Upon completing mowing of assigned tees, return to maintenance facility wash area and thoroughly clean all grass and debris from cart, walker mower, and clippings basket.
  14. After washing equipment, put away cart and basket in assigned areas.
  15. Bring walker mower to mechanic's shop (put wheels on before doing so) and leave in the designated area.
  16. Machine will be checked for quality of cut, height of cut, running condition, and cleanliness, and then refueled.

Source: Gregory J. Wojick, CGCS, Greenwich Country Club, Greenwich, Connecticut.

- Some managers feel that praise or positive feedback will be perceived as insincere. They feel uncomfortable complimenting or praising their employees.
- It takes time. Managers who are often on the run may feel that they cannot always stop to provide positive feedback.

Reasons why managers fail to deliver constructive criticism:

- Some managers avoid uncomfortable situations with employees, hoping they will "go away." Unfortunately, they tend to get worse.
- Sometimes managers think, "I don't have time to deal with that problem right now. I'll deal with it another time."
- A manager may resist giving negative feedback out of fear of being disliked by the employee.
- Sometimes managers fear the employee might resign.

The importance of both positive performance feedback and constructive criticism cannot be overstated. Employees want to know where they stand, and even the best employees appreciate compliments and praise for work well done. Likewise, immediate corrective feedback is important. If it is not provided, the employee's poor performance will be repeated and reinforced, making it more difficult to correct in the future. Providing constructive criticism becomes more comfortable when the superintendent makes it clear from the beginning of employment that both positive feedback and constructive criticism will be provided to ensure that both employee and management goals are met. This way, the employee comes to view constructive criticism as a part of the job rather than a personal attack.

Performance management as defined earlier suggests a process of working toward established performance expectations. Periodically, the manager and the employee should review the employee's performance. If it is satisfactory, praise and acknowledgment of success is appropriate to reinforce good work behavior. Many managers admit they don't provide positive feedback often enough. Authors of *The One Minute Manager* encourage supervisors to "catch your employees doing something right."

Conversely, if improvement is needed, the manager should not hesitate to discuss the areas of difficulty and coach the employee on ways to improve performance. Employee involvement in developing strategies for improved performance is also important.

For managers who feel the need to improve their coaching skills, more effective communication techniques can often provide the answer. The process described in the next section provides a practical five-step communication process for delivering performance feedback and initiating important employer-employee discussions.

REACH Method for Providing Feedback

Key Points
- Effective communication skills are essential in the coaching and feedback steps of performance appraisal.
- REACH is a tool to aid in effectively communicating performance information.
- The letters in REACH stand for the five steps in the communication process: *Rapport, Establish* purpose, *Ask* questions, *Commit* to plans, and *Highlight* plans.

Each letter in the word "REACH" stands for a step in a process of communicating your wishes to another person:

R: *Rapport.* Developing rapport involves verbal and nonverbal communication to put the person you are talking with at ease. Weather, sports, hobbies, or family are common topics.

E: *Establish* purpose. Establishing the purpose for the communication gives your discussion a clear goal. Without purpose, the other person may be reacting to the situation rather than striving to achieve established goals.

A: *Ask* questions. By asking questions and listening to the response, managers can gain additional information and ensure that the other person understands what is wanted. It is advisable to prepare questions in advance.

C: *Commit* to plans. Getting commitments to decisions and plans makes it clear to both people what steps are to be taken next. Managers should take notes as a written record for future reference.

H: *Highlight* plans. Highlighting what has been discussed and agreed upon gives the manager a chance to clarify key issues, action plans, and procedures for follow-through.

Further discussion of communication skills is the subject of Chapter 11.

The Performance Appraisal Interview

In this section we look at several key components of the performance appraisal interview, including performance appraisal mistakes, conducting a performance appraisal, and use of forms in the performance appraisal process.

Performance Appraisal Mistakes

Key Points
- Many managers stop conducting performance appraisals after several unsuccessful attempts.
- By understanding common mistakes, managers can take steps to avoid them.

The final step in the performance management process is the performance appraisal. Unfortunately, in many organizations, perceptions of performance appraisals are negative. The process becomes one of criticism and confrontation, rather than one of employee growth, development, and reward. One way to avoid common performance appraisal problems is to be aware of common mistakes. Here are some performance appraisal mistakes that often trap managers:

- **The appraisal becomes a confrontation.**

   If indeed the purpose of the performance appraisal is one of employee development and growth, it is important to avoid confrontation. Corrections in performance should have taken place through coaching and feedback during the ongoing performance management process. Use the appraisal interview to focus on employee development and the future, rather than criticize past performance.

- **The manager springs surprises on the employee.**

   Any negative behavior should be discussed and corrected at the time it occurs. Saving performance problems or issues for the appraisal interview surprises and angers the employee, and creates a "fear of the unknown" for future performance appraisals.

- **The manager sometimes acts as a judge of an individual's worth.**

  By keeping the appraisal interview performance- and behavior-oriented, there is less chance of the individual taking criticism or suggestions personally. The focus should be on the level of performance observed, the level of performance required by the position, and identification of areas for improvement.

- **The performance review is conducted with unclear goals.**

  The main goal of the appraisal should be to review past performance and discuss future expectations and plans. When performance expectations are in writing the appraisal becomes clearer.

- **The manager tries to improve too many areas of performance at one time.**

  Individuals have a tolerance limit for constructive criticism, and once this limit is met, the individual becomes increasingly upset (Caroll and Schneier, 1982). It is important to focus on one or two areas of improvement, and integrate those areas into job expectations and plans for the coming year.

- **The appraisal focuses on filling out a form rather than on actual employee performance.**

  Forms for performance appraisal are not nearly as important as the manager's relationship with the employee and the expertise the manager brings to the appraisal interview. If a form is used, it should be a management tool, rather than the focus of the performance appraisal itself.

- **Performance data are not gathered in advance.**

  If performance-related information is not gathered ahead of time, the manager may be dealing with only general instances of work behavior. The appraisal interview will become a discussion of vague issues as opposed to specific performance-related matters. When specific performance is discussed, the appraisal interview becomes more valuable.

- **Clear-cut action plans are not established.**

  An important objective of the formal appraisal is to plan future goals and performance and job expectations. Before the appraisal interview is complete, there should be some agreement between the manager and the employee regarding general performance expectations for the coming year. If necessary, a follow-up meeting can be planned to elaborate on those expectations in detail (Guinn, 1987).

Conducting a Performance Appraisal

Key Points

Use the five-step process for conducting a performance appraisal. The five steps include:
1. Explain the purpose of the discussion.
2. Elicit feedback from the employee.
3. Communicate your views regarding performance.
4. Reconcile differences.
5. Devise a plan of action for the coming employment period.

At its best, a performance appraisal is a development tool. It is an opportunity for the manager and the employee to meet and discuss performance results. Then, using those results, they can plan for the employee's growth and development in the future. At its worst, a performance appraisal interview can be a negative experience for both the employer and the employee, fraught with confrontation and criticism and mired in mistakes of the past rather than exploring opportunities for the future.

Performance evaluation should be kept simple. The purpose of the appraisal is to provide clear, useful information to employees about their performance-related behavior. Preparation for the performance appraisal interview is critical. Conduct the interview in a quiet place where both supervisor and employee will not be interrupted. Allow an adequate amount of time. Try to create as positive an atmosphere as possible and speak in positive terms during the appraisal. Before the interview, gather any written information regarding the employee's performance over the past year, and any performance expectations written at the start of the performance period.

This information should be reviewed and highlighted in the interview. If much of it has not been put in writing, the supervisor should make notes, both positive and negative, of past performance, remembering that there should be no surprises. The supervisor should also remember that the employee's tolerance for constructive criticism is limited. It is important to select only one or two areas where improvement is most needed. Avoid being too easy or too tough-minded. Be fair and honest.

To structure the performance review process and ensure that the interview is conducted completely and thoroughly, follow these steps:

1. **Explain the purpose of the discussion and the procedures that the discussion will follow**. For example, a manager might begin by indicating that the purpose of the discussion is to review the employee's performance over the past year. The beginning of the discussion may be a review of the previous performance standards, followed by a comparison of actual performance with those standards.

2. **Elicit the subordinate's ideas and opinions, making sure not to say anything that might influence or bias them**. Early in the conversation, the manager should ask for the employee's own perception of performance over the past year. If the golf course provides a performance review form, the employee can be asked to use the form for a self-evaluation of his or her performance in the past year. Effective listening and communication skills are very important in this step.

3. **Communicate your views regarding performance during the review period**. This can be based on notes or an outline that you have written. It can also be based on a performance appraisal form. If possible, it should also be based on specific performance measures that have been observed in the past year.

4. **Discuss with the subordinate any differences between the two of you and how those differences might be resolved**. During this part of the appraisal process, the manager and the employee should openly discuss any differing perceptions and come to agreement on how to resolve any differences of opinion.

5. **Together with the subordinate, devise a plan of action for carrying out whatever has been agreed upon**. This is the goal setting part of the process. After analyzing and discussing the past year's performance, place emphasis on setting performance expectations for the year to come, making those expectations measurable, time-bounded, and attainable. If the complete process cannot be carried out during the performance appraisal interview, set a separate time to finish the goal setting process for the coming performance period. End the interview by restating the positive aspects of the past year's performance and the employee's value to the business.

Use of Forms in the Appraisal Process

Large organizations with formalized personnel departments generally use forms in the performance review process. Performance appraisal rating forms provide a tool for the supervisor to conduct a complete and accurate performance appraisal. Often employees or managers may resist the use of specific forms for conducting performance appraisals. They may not like to use the forms, or they may not find them helpful for the job that they are trying to evaluate. Often, a golf course superintendent has a choice of whether to use a form or not. If a form is used, it should be designed in a way that the person conducting the appraisal can use it constructively and effectively. It is important, therefore, to be aware that several different performance appraisal forms exist and to have an understanding of why and how they are used. The following are some common approaches to preparing performance appraisal forms:

> **Comparative Procedures.** Comparative procedures are based on the relative standing of an individual among other employees. For example, comparative procedures might suggest that employee A is a better performer than employee B at a specific job, but both are better than employee C. The two most commonly used comparative procedures are straight ranking and forced distribution.
>
> 1. **Straight Ranking:** This is a simple procedure that compares a group of employees with one another. The manager typically will rank the employees from top performer in a group down to the poorest performer.
> 2. **Forced Distribution:** In this case, the manager assigns employees to a small number of categories, typically three to seven. The distribution is forced in the sense that the appraiser puts a certain percentage of employees in each category. Employees are compared to one another during the process of placing each employee in a specific category.

Comparative procedures may be useful when sorting out differences in employee performance. They are relatively easy to develop, and supervisors understand the process without too much difficulty. However, one disadvantage of comparative procedures is that they do not indicate whether an employee's performance is acceptable or unacceptable. They simply compare one worker to another.

Comparative procedures are not very helpful when employees need feedback, because they only tell the employee if performance evaluation is above or below others. They may also breed resentment among employees. Typical comparative procedures assess the overall workforce performance as opposed to specific individual performance. They tend to be global rather than specific.

Absolute standards. This approach involves determining specific standards of performance and writing them down. The person rating the performance then refers to the absolute standard to make the rating determination. The three absolute standard approaches to performance appraisal most frequently used are the trait rating scale, the behaviorally anchored rating scale, and management by objectives:

1. **The trait rating scale:** This widely used scale usually assesses general performance dimensions, such as job quality, quantity, and timeliness.

   - Performance standards are predetermined, and are usually not based on job analysis.
   - The performance standards used are often presumed to be equally applicable to a wide variety of jobs and, therefore, tend to be general in nature. For example, one performance appraisal form may be used for all jobs in a large golf club.
   - Absolute standards are judgmental by nature, and may represent different levels of performance. For example, each rater may use the same rating scale of one through five for each performance dimension. However, one individual's judgment of what constitutes a rating of five may differ from someone else's.

2. **Behaviorally anchored rating scales:** In this procedure, job behaviors are defined and integrated into a rating form. The rater then is asked to pick the description that most closely illustrates the behavior of the employee whose performance is being appraised. Behaviorally anchored rating scales are unique in that they indicate specifically and concretely the levels of performance for each performance dimension. The specific performance standards described in the rating form are designed to minimize rating errors that can occur in traditional trait rating scales. This

approach, while time-consuming, provides specific descriptions of job performance behavior.

3. **Management by objectives:** Under this approach, a set of performance objectives for the employee is established. It is expected that the objectives will be completed within a specified time period, perhaps six months or a year after their establishment. The next step in management by objectives is evaluation of the employee's performance at the end of the specified period, when the actual performance is compared with the objectives established at the beginning of the process. Management by objectives is the most individualized appraisal system. It is important for the manager to monitor this system to see that the goals established for each employee are equally challenging. This approach is very consistent with the performance management model shown in Figure 8.1.

A Word of Caution About Rating Forms

While performance appraisal forms are widely used in the business world, they should be used with caution by golf course superintendents and supervisors. A rating form or written outline is a fine tool for structuring the appraisal interview, and helping to quantify employee performance. However, it should not be used as a substitute for good communication. In the final analysis, the success of the performance appraisal depends more on the manager's execution of the whole performance management process than on the use of a particular rating form. If you don't like the rating form provided for your use, or if it interferes with the process of conducting the performance appraisal, it would be better to not use a form or to develop your own form to accomplish your performance appraisal objectives.

Summary

Properly executed, the performance management process ensures that employees understand what their job is and how well they have been performing that job. By setting performance expectations, providing feedback, and conducting annual performance appraisals, the golf course superintendent encourages peak performance. Performance management is not something that happens once a year. Rather, it is a planned, ongoing process of employee growth and development, based on continuing dialogue and feedback. Employee involvement in each step of the process will enhance employee motivation and help to ensure that the performance management process is effective.

References

Baird, L.S., R.W. Beatty, and C.E. Schneier (Eds.). 1982. The performance appraisal sourcebook. Human Resource Development Press, Amherst, MA.

Carroll, S.J. and C.E. Schneier. 1982. Performance appraisal and review systems: The identification, measurement, and development of performance in organizations. Scott Foresman and Company, Glenview, IL.

Chapman, E.N. 1986. Supervisor's survival kit. Science Research Associates, Inc., Chicago, IL.

Guinn, K. 1987. Performance management: Not just an annual appraisal. Training, August.

Friedman, M.G. 1986. 10 steps to objective appraisals. Personnel Journal 65(6):66–71.

Heneman, H.G., III, D.P. Schwab, J.A. Fossum, and L.D. Dyer. 1986. Personnel/Human resource management. Richard D. Irwin, Homewood, IL.

Hornsby, J.S. and D.F. Kuratko. 1990. Human resource management in small business: Critical issues for the 90's. Journal of Small Business Management. July.

Kirby, P.G. 1981. A systematic approach to performance appraisal. Management World 10(10:16–17), 28.

Lefton, R.E. 1985–86. Performance appraisals: Why they go wrong and how to do them right. National Productivity Review 5(1):54–63.

Malinauskas, B.K. and R.W. Clement. 1987. Performance appraisal interviewing for tangible results. Training and Development Journal 41(2): 74–9.

9

Leadership

In your position as a golf course superintendent, you are a leader. Employees look to you for direction. The board of directors and green committee turn to you for ideas and direction in developing their policies, budgets, and plans. Golfers anticipate, sometimes unrealistically, that you will always provide golf course conditions that meet their expectations.

Leadership involves crucial responsibilities and unbounded opportunities. Your success or failure as a supervisor and mentor significantly impacts the work experience and private lives of these individuals. Positive work experiences enhance professional growth and advancement possibilities and spawn positive attitudes that extend beyond the workplace. Leadership also offers the opportunity to meet and exceed the objectives of your golf course to enrich the lives of the golfer, your employees, and yourself.

This chapter is designed to help you better understand leadership and learn some tools to increase your leadership skills. But first, start thinking about leadership by answering the following questions.

- Who are several individuals you view as great leaders? They can be from history, current events, or personal experience.
- What characteristics or actions contributed to their leadership success? Why were people willing to follow them?

In our experience, frequently identified leaders include George Washington, Martin Luther King, Jr., Adolph Hitler, Abraham Lincoln, and Jesus Christ. The one characteristic common to all great leaders, by definition, is that they have followers. Academic consensus on other leadership characteristics is elusive, however.

Still, several characteristics are common to most authors' lists (Schein 1992, Cribbin 1972, Robert 1991, Locke 1991, Hitt 1988, Blanchard and Tracey 1989, and Cox 1992). These characteristics include commitment to a vision, an ability to energize and encourage others, personal integrity, and high levels of knowledge and skill.

Locke (1991) argues that effective leaders "convince [their followers] that their self-interest lies in buying into the vision that leaders have formulated and in working to implement it." Thus, the leader must first have a vision. We like to think of this vision as an attainable dream. The founding fathers of this country had a vision of freedom. Martin Luther King, Jr. had a vision of equality. Hitler had a vision of a superior race dominating the world. The early leaders of the Golf Course Superintendents Association of America must have had a vision for an effective professional organization. What were the visions of the great leaders you just identified?

Few visions can be attained by one individual. That's why leaders need followers. To keep followers pursuing the vision, leaders must encourage and energize them. Contrasting an unmotivated worker with a worker inspired by a leader's vision, Jan Carlzon concludes his book, *Moments of Truth,* with the following story (Carlzon 1987):

"A visitor to a stone quarry asked two workers what they were doing.

"The first stone cutter, looking rather sour, grumbled, 'I'm cutting this damned stone into a block.'

"The second, who looked pleased with his work, replied proudly, 'I'm on a team that's building a cathedral.'"

Reflect on how the great leaders you selected energized and encouraged their followers.

Leaders with personal integrity make decisions and commitments with honesty and conviction, and then always follow through. They never view any commitment or person as unimportant. In discussing personal integrity, Blanchard and Tracey (1989) suggest making every decision as though it would be a headline in the local paper.

Vision, energy, and integrity are not enough to gain the respect of followers. Effective leaders also must have knowledge and skill. The leader must understand the organization's operation, and have excellent communication and interpersonal skills. Assess the knowledge and skill level of the great leaders you identified.

Your leadership responsibilities as a golf course superintendent have two major components. First, there is the matter of establishing direction for your staff. This involves developing a vision for the golf course and securing the commitment of your staff to the vision. The second component involves enabling every member of your staff to participate in attaining the vision. High levels of both vision and implementation are required to be an effective leader or manager (Hitt 1988). Without vision, the golf course superintendent is a doer without committed employees. Lacking implementation skills, the superintendent is a dreamer with no mechanism to make the vision a reality.

Take a few moments now to analyze your personal strengths and weaknesses in these four characteristics of leadership:

Characteristic	Rating (check one for each characteristic)			
	Fair	Good	Excellent	Outstanding
Vision				
Motivation				
Integrity				
Knowledge				

With this self-analysis complete, you are ready to learn new tools for improving your leadership skills.

Leadership Defined

Key Points
- Leadership is any behavior that develops or uses power to influence other peoples' behavior.
- The various sources of power should be selected appropriately as resources to influence followers.

Leadership can be defined as any behavior that develops or uses power in order to influence other peoples' behavior. Leadership is used by management to achieve enthusiastic, willing, zealous participation of followers to accomplish the organization's mission and objectives. This definition includes three key terms: behavior, influence, and power.

Behavior is any action or group of actions. As noted earlier, leadership is not an inborn quality; rather, it is the use of specific skills—skills that can be learned and improved.

Influence is the ability to affect the behavior of others. It is the catalyst through which leadership actions are successful.

We will discuss power shortly, but first let's consider an example. You are providing the leadership needed to convince a candidate for Assistant Golf Course Superintendent to accept the job offer. You have a plan of action you hope will influence the candidate to accept the job. The plan contains your behaviors. You hope this behavior will influence the candidate's behavior concerning the job acceptance decision.

The resource you use to influence the candidate is **power**. Power is given willingly by followers in expectation of the leader meeting their needs. Another example brings the definition of power to life and illustrates the various sources of power.

The annual member/guest tournament is coming up. Since you can't get everything ready by yourself, you must influence many people to help. In exerting this leadership, you use many forms of power.

You undoubtedly rely on the **formal power** that is attached to the position of golf course superintendent to make assignments to maintenance staff. But the use of formal power alone almost never provides effective or sufficient leadership. You also have access to an array of informal bases of power, including expert power, information power, personal power, reward power, connection power, and coercive power.

By explaining how precise maintenance impacts green speed, you use your **expert power** to convince the green committee to appropriate extra funds to enable you to pay your staff overtime wages to ensure that the course is in exceptional condition.

With your awareness of the provisions of the Americans with Disabilities Act, you can wield **information power** in persuading the general manager to make certain that course and clubhouse restrooms meet accessibility guidelines.

You may capitalize on your personality and charm—aspects of **personal power**—to enlist volunteers to help with cleanup after the big event.

Your employees are happy to put forth that extra effort for excellence, anticipating your personal words of praise and the special party you're planning in recognition of their hard work, long hours, and devotion. Both are forms of **reward power**. You gained the reward power for the party by cashing in on your **connection power**—the strong rapport you share with the general manager, who found some money in the budget and asked the club manager to arrange an employee barbecue.

When a vendor gives you the runaround on why the special golf flags you ordered for the tournament were not delivered on schedule, you decide to exert your **coercive power**. You let the sales representative know that you will be contacting the regional sales manager, and if you don't get satisfaction, you will take your business elsewhere.

Figure 9.1 contains specific definitions of these sources of power. The sources are listed generally from the most directive to the most empowering. A leader achieves maximal effectiveness by tailoring their use to the situation at hand. Formal power is not the only source of power. In fact, use of formal power alone almost never provides effective leadership. The golf course superintendent should strive to increase the use of empowering power sources while reducing reliance on more directive sources, particularly coercive and formal power.

Figure 9.1. Forms of Power

Formal power is based on the position held by the leader. A leader with formal power induces compliance from or influences others because the employee feels that this person has the right, by virtue of position in the organization, to expect that instructions or suggestions be followed.
Coercive power is based on fear. A leader using coercive power often resorts to punishment, reprimands, or dismissal. Dictatorships almost always survive primarily through the use of coercive power.
Connection power is based on the leader's connections with influential or important persons inside or outside the organization. A leader who demonstrates connection power induces cooperation from others because they wish to gain favor or avoid the disfavor of the powerful connection.
Reward power is based on the leader's ability to reward people. Followers believe that their cooperation leads to gaining positive incentives, such as promotions or recognition.
Personal power is based on the leader's personal traits. A leader high in personal power is generally liked and admired by others because of personality. This liking for, admiration of, and identification with the leader influences others.
Information power is based on the leader's access to information that is valuable to others. This power base influences others because employees need this information or want to be let "in" on things. Early access to financial information is an example of information power.
Expert power is based on the leader's possession of expertise, skill, and knowledge which, through respect, influences others. A leader with expert power is seen as possessing the expertise to improve the work behavior of others.

Leadership Styles

Key Points
- Coercive, authoritative, affiliative, democratic, pacesetting, and empowering styles are used by leaders.
- Effective leaders use the styles most appropriate to the situation.

When you select a grass seed mixture for a particular location on the golf course, you consider the characteristics of the location and of the seed varieties. Similarly, in leadership, you have alternative "varieties" or styles to use depending upon the situation, the characteristics of the employee, and your own leadership capabilities. The six leadership styles—coercive, authoritative, affiliative, democratic, pacesetting, and empowering—are your leadership "varieties." The six can be described as follows:

Coercive: Managers with this style tend to expect immediate compliance with their directions and solicit little or no input. They manage by controlling subordinates tightly and tend to influence with discipline.

Authoritative: Managers who use this style are often referred to as "firm but fair." They tend to manage by providing clear instructions, soliciting some input (while leaving no doubt as to who is boss), monitoring behavior, and motivating with both discipline and rewards. They see influence as a key part of the manager's job.

Affiliative: Managers with this as their dominant leadership style tend to feel people come first and tasks second. They see the manager's job as one of maintaining a pleasant working environment and providing job security and other benefits. They want to be liked and they tend to provide little direction, especially feedback about unsatisfactory performance.

Democratic: These managers are known for their participative style. They tend to believe that individuals and groups function best when allowed to work together and, therefore, tend to feel that close supervision or very detailed instructions are not necessary. Democratic managers tend to hold many meetings, they reward adequate performance, and they dislike disciplining employees.

Pacesetting: These managers like to perform technical activities as well as manage. They have very high standards for themselves and expect the same of others. These managers usually expect their employees to develop a keen sense of personal responsibility. They often have little concern for interpersonal relations and may reassign work if employee ability or willingness hampers performance.

Empowering: Empowering managers see themselves as developing their employees and have high standards of performance. They delegate authority and allow followers flexibility in setting goals and completing tasks.

These styles are a complete leadership toolbox. Studying the advantages and disadvantages of each will help you better understand the proper use of each (Figure 9.2).

It is natural to rely on the two or three leadership tools that you are most comfortable with, but with study, practice, and planning, you can become comfortable with all six. First, you must recognize the styles you most prefer. You should answer these two questions:

1. Which styles am I comfortable with?
2. Which styles don't seem right to me?

The styles you are comfortable with are your default styles. In situations where you have not taken the time to plan a leadership strategy, you are almost certain to use one of your default styles. However, if you analyze circumstances more carefully, you begin to recognize situations where less comfortable leadership styles are best. Just as seeding of less familiar varieties requires more study and planning, effective use of uncomfortable styles requires that you plan for and concentrate on implementing the selected style.

Leadership in Practice

Key Points
- Actions involving employees include task and supporting behaviors.
- Situational leadership applies appropriate degrees of task and supporting behaviors.

Golf course superintendents don't set one irrigation schedule and run it forever. They seek to apply water efficiently and effectively by considering factors such as the weather, the evapotranspiration rate, and the infiltration rate. Similarly, an effective leader applies a particular leadership approach only after considering the situation at hand. To determine what is appropriate, the leader must gauge the employee/follower's needs along two primary dimensions. The first deals primarily with job tasks. The second concerns the employee's/follower's feelings and attitudes, including commitment to the job and the club.

Figure 9.2. Leadership Styles Pros and Cons

Style	Advantages	Disadvantages
Coercive	• Short term efficiency—fast • Clear line of authority—know who is in charge and desired action is usually taken	• Most people don't like it • Inhibits employee growth and development • May lead to high staff turnover
Authoritative	• Efficient • Clear who is in charge • A way of exercising power without intimidation	• Not conducive to personal growth and development • Some people may not like it • Can lead to turnover
Affiliative	• Keeps people happy (short run) • Allows people freedom	• Change is avoided • Change becomes a source of conflict • Low productivity • Decisions may not be in best interest of the organization • Little encouragement for personal growth

Style	Advantages	Disadvantages
Democratic	• Involves people • Opportunities for growth	• Time-consuming • Antagonist may sabotage organizational goals • Majority decisions aren't always in the best interest of the organization
Pacesetting	• Can be productive—short term • Works well with committed followers	• Doesn't work well with unwilling or unable followers • Followers may not follow • Problems in absence of the pacesetters
Empowering	• Encourages growth and development • Long-term productivity • People respond well	• Time-consuming • Costs are high if you have high turnover due to the development investment that is lost

For example, if the leader notes that an employee has not mastered a particular task, the leader must provide a high level of leadership in "task behavior." Conversely, if the employee has the task down pat, only a low level of "task behavior" leadership is needed.

Similarly, if the leader senses a need for building the employee's commitment and confidence, he or she must provide a high level of "supporting behavior."

These two dimensions of leadership are central to the concept of situational leadership developed by Blanchard and Hersey (Hersey and Blanchard, 1988; Blanchard, Zigarmi, and Zigarmi, 1985). The golf course superintendent can use situational leadership to match an appropriate leadership approach to the developmental level of the employee, similar to selecting a varietal mixture to match the characteristics of the seedbed.

Figure 9.3 shows the intensity of the leader's task behaviors on one axis and the intensity of supporting behaviors on the other, producing four quadrants that correspond to four situational leadership approaches:

- **Directive** (high in "task" leadership; low in "supporting" leadership)—This approach is desirable when all of the power rests in the leader and the overriding emphasis is on getting the job done. Appropriate uses include crisis and orientation.

- **Coaching** (high in "task" leadership; high in "supporting" leadership)—The leader uses this style to build commitment while providing training and/or direction. Feedback and support are necessary, as the employee has not yet mastered the task or become committed to the club.

- **Supporting** (low in "task" leadership; high in "supporting" leadership)—After concluding that the task has been mastered, the leader uses this approach to build the employee's commitment and confidence.

- **Delegating** (low in "task" leadership; low in "supporting" leadership)—The leader uses this approach when the employee has the commitment and confidence to independently set and accomplish the goals necessary to successfully fulfill the assigned responsibilities.

The four quadrants can also be viewed as sections of a continuum, along which followers can progress from needing first directive leadership, then coaching, then supporting, until they finally are ready to accept delegation. The leader's effectiveness, in terms of progress in attaining the organization's visionary goals, is enhanced by encouraging each follower to advance as far as possible along the continuum.

Figure 9.3. Situational Leadership Model

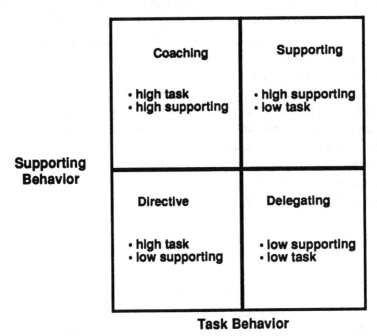

The supervisor's challenge is thus twofold. First, to determine which leadership approach is appropriate for a particular employee's situation, and then to enable the employee to progress as far toward delegating as is desirable, given his or her individual capabilities and job responsibilities.

But what do you do when you find that an employee is not succeeding with the approach you are using? The solution to this problem is to retrace the path to the quadrant in which the employee can succeed at the particular task. Thus, if a delegating approach is failing, begin by increasing your supporting behavior—encouragement, positive feedback, and reward. This supporting quadrant is a crucial, but often neglected, component of the development. When the employee knows the task but has not yet developed the attitudes and commitment to accept complete delegation of the task, he or she needs high levels of supporting behavior.

Only if supporting behavior fails to correct the problem should you introduce task behaviors (coaching). Just as you must allow each employee to advance through the quadrants one at a time, it is crucial not to skip quadrants if you must retrace. Many strong employer-employee relationships have been severely damaged by the supervisor becoming directive upon concluding that the supporting or delegating approach is not working.

In addressing golf course superintendent leadership, we have discussed leadership styles, sources of power, and situational leadership. For each quadrant of situational leadership, particular power sources are likely to be more useful and certain leadership styles are likely to be more effective. For example, in a crisis (directive quadrant), the superintendent relies on the formal power of his or her position, and probably invokes a coercive or authoritative leadership style. When utilizing a coaching approach, the superintendent is likely to use an authoritative style while relying on formal, expert, and information power. In contrast, reward and/or personal power are likely to be employed through an affiliative or democratic style of leadership when using a supporting approach. In delegating situations, the superintendent should use the empowering and pacesetting styles while using personal and expert when appropriate.

Summary

As a golf course manager, you are a leader, and are expected to provide direction for the people in your organization, while enabling them to achieve success in your organization's plans and visions. These followers are crucial to your successful attainment of the golf course's mission and vision.

Successful leadership is achieved through the use of power to influence others. The types of power range from coercive to reward to personal, and leaders should have the full palette of power types available to them. Depending upon the situation you are facing and your personal leadership style, you should choose the most appropriate power type.

Your leadership style should also vary based on the employee that you are interacting with and your own leadership characteristics. These leadership styles also run the gamut, from coercive to empowering. Situational leadership is an approach based on two dimensions of leadership behaviors—task behaviors and supporting behaviors. By striking the right balance of task and supporting behaviors for the specific employee that needs guidance, you effectively match your leadership style to the developmental level of the employee, thereby increasing the effectiveness of your interaction.

With effective leadership, the golf course superintendent can positively influence both productivity and interpersonal relationships. Selection and planning of appropriate leadership approaches for each staff member is just as important to a high-quality golf course as selection and nurturing of the mixture of varieties of grasses.

References

Blanchard, K. and B. Tracey. 1989. Blanchard and Tracey on leadership. Blanchard Training and Development, Escondido, CA.

Blanchard, K., P. Zigarmi, and D. Zigarmi. 1985. Leadership and the one minute manager. William Morrow and Company, New York, NY.

Carlzon, J. 1987. Moments of truth. Ballinger Publishing Company, Cambridge, MA.

Covey, S.R. 1989. The seven habits of highly effective people: Restoring the character ethic. Simon and Schuster, New York, NY.

Cribbin, J.J. 1972. Effective managerial leadership. American Management Association.

Cox, D. 1992. Leadership when the heat's on. McGraw-Hill, New York.

Franklin International Institute. 1989. Franklin Day planner system: Guidebook. Franklin International Institute, Salt Lake City, UT.

Hersey, P. and K. Blanchard. 1988. Management of organizational behavior: Utilizing human resources. Prentice Hall, Englewood Cliffs, NJ.

Hitt, W.D. 1988. The leader-manager: Guidelines for action. Battelle Press, Columbia, OH.

Locke, E.A. 1991. The essence of leadership: the four keys of leading successfully. Lexington Books, New York, NY.

McClelland, D. 1975. A handbook of structural experiences for human relations training. Vol. V. University Associates Press, Iowa City, IA.

Robert, M. 1991. The essence of leadership: strategy, innovation, and decisiveness. Quorum Books, New York, NY.

Schein, E.H. 1992. Organizational culture and leadership, 2nd ed. Jossey-Bass Publishers, San Francisco, CA.

10

Employee Motivation

Many managers have been frustrated at one time or another by unmotivated employees. Some managers ask "Why can't I motivate my people?" The answer lies in the fact that no one can motivate another person. Motivation comes from within each of us. **Motivation is the willingness to put forth effort in pursuit of goals based on individual wants and needs**. If we accept the fact that motivation comes from within each individual, then the role of the manager in employee motivation becomes one of creating a work environment where employees are motivated to pursue the goals of the organization while achieving their own goals as well.

When golf course superintendents get together and talk about what motivates their employees, there is often lively debate about the extent to which money motivates. It is true in our society that we work in order to live, support ourselves, and attain a reasonable quality of life. In addition, we want to know that our efforts are noticed, that we are making a contribution, and that the work we do is appreciated. Everyone wants recognition and appreciation for their work. Managers, however, often do not recognize the importance of these factors in day-to-day motivation of their staff. Indeed, there are employees who would say "enough with the praise and appreciation, just fatten my paycheck," but a few words of praise and appreciation last much longer in the minds of most employees than an increase in pay. One of the superintendent's challenges is to determine the rewards—financial or otherwise—that employees appreciate most and then to provide those rewards to create a motivational work environment.

Motivation: A Historical Perspective

Researchers and educators have proposed numerous ways of viewing motivation. Perhaps the most popular of these are Maslow's "Hierarchy of

121

Needs," and Frederick Herzberg's "Two-Factor Theory." To more clearly focus on the components of motivation as they relate to golf course superintendents, let's look at both of these theories.

Key Points

- Motivational theories provide a framework for thinking about employee motivation.
- Abraham Maslow identified five needs that impact human motivation: physical needs, safety needs, social needs, esteem needs, and self-actualization needs.
- Frederick Herzberg believed that there were two types of factors affecting human motivation: maintenance factors, which can only prevent dissatisfaction, and motivation factors.

Abraham Maslow—The Hierarchy of Needs

In the early 1950s, Abraham Maslow was one of the first psychologists to study the positive aspects of human behavior. Prior to this time, much of the study of psychology centered around mental illness and other psychological problems. Maslow studied human behavior as it related to motivation and proposed the hierarchy of needs to explain human motivation (Figure 10.1). He identified five human needs that impact an individual's motivation. Maslow further stated that an individual is likely to satisfy the most basic human needs first (starting at the bottom of the pyramid), and then move up to the next order of needs.

Following are the needs that Maslow identified, starting with the most basic:

1. *Physical needs*—These are the lowest order of needs, and include things such as food, clothing, shelter, and comfort. In terms of working conditions, this order of needs includes a pleasant work environment, adequate pay and benefits, work breaks, and labor-saving devices.
2. *Safety needs*—These needs include security for oneself and one's position, and avoidance of risk, harm, and pain. Translated into job-related needs, these include safe working conditions, proper supervision, retirement programs, and assurances of job security.

Figure 10.1.

Maslow's Hierarchy of Needs

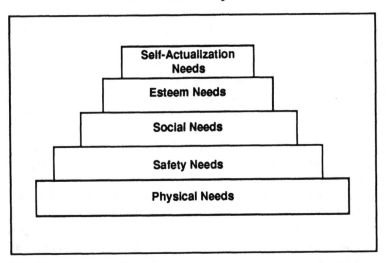

Source: Plunkett, W. Richard, *Supervision: The Direction of People at Work,* Second Edition. 1979, William C. Brown Company Publishers, Dubuque, IA, pp. 112–116.

3. *Social needs*—Social needs include companionship, acceptance by others, love and affection, and the feeling of group membership. Managers meet these needs on the job by creating opportunities for interaction with others, building a team spirit, and creating a work environment that is friendly and enjoyable.

4. *Esteem needs*—These needs include responsibility, self-respect, recognition by others, and a sense of accomplishment. On the job, these needs take the form of status symbols, such as seniority, job title, award programs, challenging work, participation in decisionmaking, and the opportunity for advancement within the business.

5. *Self-actualization needs*—The highest order of human needs that Maslow identified is self-actualization. These needs include reaching your potential as an individual, independence, creativity, and self-expression. On the job, these needs may be filled by involvement in work planning, freedom to make decisions affecting the work, creativity in performing the work and opportunities for growth and development on the job.

From a practical standpoint, Maslow's needs hierarchy is helpful if we consider that employees vary in their needs at any given point in time. Consider the following case example:

> Bill Murphy is 21 years old, single, and has been working at the Successful Valley Country Club for the past three years. He has a high school education, very good mechanical skills, and a strong work ethic. Bill's main interests in life outside of his job are hunting, fishing, and snowmobiling. Although he has always been one to party on the weekends, his weekend social activities don't interfere with his work.
>
> Bill lives in an apartment in town and his main asset is a new four-wheel-drive vehicle he recently purchased and is paying for in hefty monthly payments.
>
> Bill's employer, Jim Lewis, values him and wants to keep him happy and satisfied. At times Jim has offered benefits that some of the other employees receive, including health insurance and a pension plan. Each time the issue has been brought up, Bill simply says that he likes working at the golf course, he would like to work there a long time, and that he wants the cash to make his truck payments and do the other things he enjoys.

In this case, Bill appears to be at the physical needs level of Maslow's need hierarchy, wanting money to meet his basic needs. Assume that as Bill gets older, he buys a home, gets married, and has a family. His safety and security needs will change and he will move up the need hierarchy. By assessing an employee's position on the need hierarchy, an employer can better determine those things that are likely to motivate.

The Two-Factor Theory of Dr. Frederick Herzberg

In the late 1950's, Dr. Frederick Herzberg further evolved Maslow's motivational concepts. He developed a theory based on two sets of factors that provide motivation in the workplace.

Maintenance Factors

The first set of factors is called maintenance or hygiene factors. They provide for the employee's basic needs. Herzberg suggested that these factors do not necessarily create a motivated workforce, but he indicated that a lack of them would cause dissatisfaction among employees:

1. *Economic factors*—These include wages, insurance, vacation, retirement, and a variety of other fringe benefits.
2. *Security needs*—Security factors include grievance procedures, seniority privileges, fair work rules, company policies, and discipline.
3. *Social needs*—These needs include opportunities to mix with one's peers. Examples include: business sponsorship of parties, outings, and work breaks.
4. *Working conditions*—These include adequate heat, light, ventilation, and reasonable hours of work—both length of work week and hours per day.
5. *Status*—These issues would include privileges, job titles, and other symbols of rank and position.

Herzberg suggested that if the maintenance or hygiene factors are inadequate or not provided at all, employees are likely to become dissatisfied. If the employee considers these factors adequate, they are thought to prevent dissatisfaction rather than create any appreciable level of motivation. Herzberg felt that the failure to provide these factors would result in job dissatisfaction and reduced productivity.

Think about what you hear golf course employees on your and other courses complain about. It's a good bet that there is a strong relationship between what you come up with and the maintenance or hygiene factors.

Motivation Factors

Motivation factors are the second set of factors identified by Herzberg. When provided in the proper quantity and quality, these factors have the potential to satisfy the employee's needs and create an increased commitment of time and energy to the job. Motivation factors can make the difference between a highly motivated worker and one who is just marginally motivated, according to Herzberg. Motivation factors include:

1. *Challenging work*—People want to view their job as offering opportunities for self-expression and growth. People tend to need goals or challenges to stretch their abilities and performance.
2. *Feeling of personal accomplishment*—Employees tend to get a sense of achievement and feeling of contribution when presented with a task at which they can succeed.

3. *Recognition for achievement*—Employees want to feel that their contributions have been worth the effort and that the effort has been acknowledged and appreciated.

4. *Achievement of increasing responsibility*—Employees want to acquire new duties and responsibilities. This can be accomplished by expanding a job or by delegating more responsibility to an employee.

5. *A sense of importance to the organization*—Employees want to feel that their presence is needed and that their individual contributions are necessary and make a difference in the business.

6. *Access to information*—Employees want to know about the things that affect them and their jobs. They want to be kept informed through proper communication channels.

7. *Involvement in decisionmaking*—Most employees desire a voice in what goes on in the workplace, particularly in terms of input on important decisions. They want and need the freedom to exercise initiative and creativity.

Now think about what you like about your own job. It's a good bet that there is a strong relationship between your list and these factors. These are the things we and our employees like about our jobs and that correspondingly produce commitment and motivation. Figure 10.2 shows the contrast between Herzberg's maintenance factors and motivation factors.

Maslow's hierarchy of needs and Herzberg's two-factor theory are only two of many frameworks for motivation that have been offered by researchers and academics. They are discussed here to familiarize you with some different ways motivation has been viewed. While theoretical in nature, these two frameworks help provide a basis for considering the more practical aspects of motivation as it relates to golf course superintendents and their supervisors.

Compensation and Motivation

Key Points
- Compensation is an important aspect of motivation.
- Compensation should be competitive with that offered by other employers.

Figure 10.2.

Herzberg's Two-Factor Theory	
Hygiene or Maintenance Factors	**Motivation Factors**
1. Economic Factors	1. Challenging Work
2. Security Needs	2. Feeling of Personal Accomplishment
3. Social Needs	3. Recognition for Achievement
4. Working Conditions	4. Achievement of Increasing Re-sponsibility
5. Status	5. Importance of the Organization
	6. Access to Information
	7. Involvement in Decisionmaking

Source: Plunkett, W. Richard, *Supervision: The Direction of People at Work, 2nd Edition.* 1979, William C. Brown Company Publishers, Dubuque, IA, pp. 123-126.

No discussion of motivation would be complete without addressing the importance of compensation issues. Compensation is the exchange of pay in the form of wages and benefits in return for work. It is beyond the scope of this book to provide a complete discussion of all the aspects of compensation. However, given the fact that compensation directly impacts employee motivation, recruiting, and other aspects of employment, it is important to consider the key issues related to compensation.

A golf course functions because people are willing to exchange their time, knowledge, skills, and effort for money and other rewards that a job offers. Compensation can mean many things to an employee. But for the most part, it is a means to a livelihood, to having the comforts that life has to offer. In some cases, higher pay levels lead to feelings of self-worth and status. The primary goal of a compensation plan is to help employers attract, retain, and motivate capable employees. To accomplish this goal, the compensation plan should meet the following criteria:

1. The compensation plan must be competitive with those of other businesses in the local labor market. Golf course superintendents in an area must not only compete with other golf course super-intendents in their own geographic area, but also with the rest of the business community as well.
2. The time, cost, and energy devoted to the compensation plan should be reasonable. For golf courses, the system should be relatively simple and easily understood by both employer and

employee. It should also be comprehensive enough to address a range of employee needs.

3. The compensation program should be fair. Employees must understand the compensation policies and believe that they are impartially administered. Claims of inequity in pay between employees are one of the more common compensation difficulties that employers confront. The compensation plan must provide evidence that comparability has been considered. It should also be clear to employees what they must do to earn more.

4. The compensation plan should meet the varying needs of employees. People value different aspects of compensation based on individual needs. People's needs differ according to their family situations, values, and perspectives. These should be taken into account as compensation plans are developed.

Components of Compensation

Compensation generally has three parts: wages, benefits, and perquisites:

1. *Wages*—Wages are the cash amount regularly paid for meeting the requirements of a job. It is usually close to the market value of that particular job.

2. *Benefits*—Benefits are the fixed portion of pay, and include things such as insurance, vacation, retirement programs, unemployment insurance, workers' compensation insurance, etc. Benefits can have an extremely high value to employees, particularly health insurance.

3. *Perquisites*—"Perks" are the individualized benefits that set individuals, often managers, apart. Some can have great value, both financial and motivational. Perks may include use of a golf course vehicle to drive, use of the golf course at non-peak times, use of golf club facilities, dining privileges, and other special privileges. Perquisites can make a given job more attractive.

Providing Competitive Compensation

If the compensation package is going to aid in attracting the most qualified employees, it must be competitive. To ensure a competitive compensation package, the manager must know what competing businesses and industries are providing in both wages and benefits.

In large corporations, this is commonly done through the use of compensation surveys. In developing a compensation survey, the business makes a series of decisions regarding what to study. Decisions include the purpose of the study, what types of jobs to survey, what geographical area to cover, and what businesses to contact.

From a practical standpoint, there are important differences between the ability of large industries and golf courses to conduct compensation surveys. Large firms often allocate substantial budgets to their human resource management divisions and may also be able to afford to hire outside professionals to conduct extensive surveys. While the management of a golf course may not have the time or financial resources to conduct large-scale compensation surveys, some information must be gathered to determine compensation competitiveness.

While some industry-wide surveys may be available, ultimately it becomes the manager's responsibility to do the local information gathering. This can be done by conducting a small telephone survey of golf courses in your area. It is also important to contact non-golf course businesses in the area, since some are competing for the same labor pool. Determining compensation competitiveness can be difficult in some cases, but it is an important managerial function when setting up compensation packages that will attract the best people.

Creating A Motivational Work Environment

Key Points
The manager's role in motivation is to provide a work environment where employees will be peak performers. This is done by:
- Hiring individuals with the potential to achieve.
- Considering individual wants and needs.
- Setting a good example.

Having considered what Maslow and Herzberg said about motivation, a reasonable question to ask is, "How does a manager create an environment where employees are satisfied and motivated?" The following three steps are keys to creating a motivational work environment on the golf course. The incentive to create this environment, of course, is greater employee satisfaction, productivity, and a higher level of business success.

1. Hire individuals with the potential to achieve

The manager's motivational job begins with the recruitment of highly qualified people. Researchers suggest that the most productive workers are at least three times as productive as the least productive workers. Hiring the best available workers increases the manager's chances of building a highly motivated workforce. Hiring poor workers makes the manager's motivational job difficult, if not impossible. It is better to invest extra time in the recruiting process to find the "right" person for the job than to try to motivate the "wrong" person.

2. Consider the wants and needs of the individual

Employees are individuals with different characteristics and personal values. Rewards that satisfy one employee do not necessarily satisfy or motivate another. Getting to know people as individuals and providing for their wants and needs improves the motivational climate of the organization. For some employees this may take the form of wages or specific benefits. For other employees, valued rewards may include increased responsibility and recognition for specific achievements or promotion.

Figure 10.3 highlights the importance of recognizing the wants and needs of employees. This figure summarizes research work conducted by the Labor Relations Institute of New York in 1986. It lists ten potentially motivating job factors, indicates how employees ranked each factor, and gives the supervisor's perception of how the employee would rank each factor. Note how differently the managers' responses were from the employees' responses. This example highlights the importance of continuous communication with employees to stay in touch with the types of rewards each employee values.

3. Set a good example

To create a motivational work environment for the people you supervise, you must be motivated yourself. Motivation principles apply to golf course superintendents and supervisors just as they do to employees. As a superintendent, you should think about the things that motivate you and the things that help you to become motivated in your own work. The superintendent who has his or her own personal goals and is organized and enthusiastic about his or her work will be better prepared to create the type of environment where others will be motivated to pursue work goals and achieve success.

Figure 10.3

What People Want from their Work		
Job Factors	**Employee Ranking**	**Supervisor Ranking**
Interesting work	1	5
Full appreciation of work done	2	8
Feeling of being in on things	3	10
Job security	4	2
Good wages	5	1
Promotion and growth in the organization	6	3
Good working conditions	7	4
Personal loyalty to employees	8	7
Sympathetic help with personal problems	9	9
Tactful discipline	10	6

Source: Kenneth A. Korvach, "Why Motivational Theories Don't Work," *S.A.M. Advance Management Journal,* Spring 1980, pp. 56–59.

Keys to Unlocking Motivation in Golf Course Employees

Key Points
- There are many practical things a golf course superintendent can do every day to encourage employee motivation.
- By learning and following the 10 keys to unlocking employee motivation, the manager can improve employee work performance and job satisfaction.

Every manager wants to know what specific things can be done to motivate his or her employees. Now that we have looked at motivation theory, the role of wages and benefits, and creating a motivational environment, let's look at some specific things you can do to motivate your employees.

1. Provide praise and positive feedback

A golf course superintendent or supervisor should never underestimate the power of sincere praise and appreciation as a motivator. We all need to be appreciated, needed, and valued by others. Sincere appreciation expressed to employees for their accomplishments makes the individual feel good and want to continue to perform at a high level. All too often managers reprimand and provide negative feedback without taking the time and effort to look for the things that employees are doing well and to praise them. The issue of giving employees positive and negative feedback can be viewed as an "emotional bank account." Praise, recognition, and feedback represent deposits in the emotional bank account. Conversely, constructive criticism or reprimands can be viewed as withdrawals from the emotional bank account. It is obvious from this analogy that if the supervisor is continually correcting or reprimanding an employee and providing minimal, if any, positive feedback, praise, or appreciation, the result is being "overdrawn" on the emotional bank account. Employees can accept reprimands and constructive criticism if they are confident that their work is truly appreciated and that they are making a contribution to the organization.

2. Delegate responsibility

The delegation of responsibility and authority in itself is a powerful incentive to produce motivated employees. As a manager's responsibility grows and develops, the use of delegation is critical for accomplishing more through people and providing for employees' personal growth and development. Many managers find delegation difficult for a variety of reasons. The manager has to relinquish some control over how things are done. There is a tendency to feel that if responsibilities are delegated, the manager becomes less important. It is important for golf course superintendents to remember that delegation of power is not a zero-sum game. In other words, if the superintendent delegates some power to an employee, it doesn't mean that the superintendent has less; what it really means is that through delegation, the entire organization has more. The more people are empowered to accept responsibility, the greater the potential for unlocking the talent of each individual. Delegation of responsibility and authority to make decisions, however, should not be given lightly. The employee must show the ability and desire to accept new responsibilities and, most important, it must be clear to both the manager and the employee that the employee is accountable for carrying out the assigned responsibilities.

3. Help employees set goals

Researchers Locke and Latham have clearly shown that employees who have work-related goals accomplish more than those employees who do not. Research has also shown that it does not matter if the employer sets the goal or the employee sets his or her own goals; the most important issue in goal setting is that an attainable goal is set. It should also be remembered that, when the employee sets the goals there is usually more commitment to those goals. Another issue in goal setting is that employees tend to set more difficult goals than they can reasonably achieve. Working with employees to set realistic and rewarding goals results in greater motivation. It is the achievement of challenging yet attainable goals that provides the motivation for the next work assignment.

4. Provide encouragement

At first, providing encouragement may sound a lot like providing praise and positive feedback. However, there is an important difference. Praise and positive feedback are given after someone has achieved something valuable and worthwhile in their work—in short, after someone has done a good job. Encouragement, on the other hand, comes prior to someone tackling or completing a challenging task. Employees who feel that their supervisor has confidence in them and strongly supports their efforts in completing a tough assignment are far more likely to have the confidence to complete the assignment than an employee who is not encouraged and supported by his or her supervisor.

5. Make careful use of compensation

Clearly there are times when increases in pay for good performance or an increase in benefits will be particularly appreciated by an employee, especially in a case where compensation is provided as a reward for performance. Conduct salary surveys of golf courses and other employers in your area to determine what different positions are paying relative to your own. A salary survey can be as simple as a series of phone calls to help determine what competitors are paying in the current season. After the salary survey is conducted, be sure you are paying competitively. Once competitive pay rates are established, be sure to provide reasonable raises. Small raises can be demotivating if they are seen as insignificant. Also, avoid giving equal raises to all employees. Try to vary raises with the performance of individuals or the importance of the job. Above all, try to develop compensation as much as possible as a reward system for good performance.

6. Recognize the best employees with promotion or advancement

Some golf courses are large enough to provide several steps on a career ladder over time. On other courses, the golf course maintenance staff is smaller and there is relatively little room for formal job advancement. Regardless of whether the staff is large or small, attempts should be made to offer advancement where it is feasible. In a larger organization, it is often possible to promote a good worker to a position like Assistant Golf Course Superintendent. In a smaller organization, perhaps the advancement would take the form of skill development. For example, there is a certain amount of prestige and status that comes from operating larger, more advanced mowers and pieces of golf course equipment. Training a good performer to operate more expensive and sophisticated pieces of equipment is, in itself, a form of elevation in responsibility and can be a strong motivator.

7. Make the individual's job as meaningful as possible

Mundane, repetitive, and simplistic work often leads to monotony and boredom for the person who has to do it. Try to include some new assignments along with the basic routine work. Some superintendents rotate jobs so an individual is not doing the exact same job every single day. Provide learning opportunities that allow employees to grow and develop a sense of pride in their work. Finally, one of the most important ways to create meaningful work on the golf course is to clearly let employees know why they are doing a particular job and why it is important to the course and to the people who play the course. Employees who feel that the tasks that they do each day are valued by someone have more pride in their work and greater motivation.

8. Provide the best working conditions possible

Working conditions can have a major impact on how happy and satisfied people are in their work. The fact that golf course maintenance is outdoor work attracts many people to the job. However, not all aspects of outdoor work are desirable at all times. Weather conditions, for example, can have a major impact on employee morale and productivity. Consider the employee who attempts to do his job during the fifth day of a heat wave in the middle of the summer, or the employee who is only half as productive in rainy weather as he is in good weather. Make adjustments in working conditions whenever and wherever possible to improve employee morale and productivity. Be sure all workers have the protective clothing they need: rain gear, gloves for heavy work, or respirators when they are using pesticides or other toxic material. Be sure equipment is in good repair and is easy to operate.

Work hours are also considered a part of working conditions. Allowing employees flexible work times that meet their personal schedules can be a major motivator. Also, allowing for work to start earlier on days of extreme heat or other weather conditions can make a difference. By tuning in to difficult working conditions and trying to make adjustments to improve those conditions, golf course superintendents and supervisors greatly improve staff morale and productivity.

9. Involve employees in decisionmaking

Employee involvement can be a powerful motivational tool. It is not appropriate to involve employees in making every decision regarding golf course maintenance; many decisions can only be made by the golf course superintendent. For example, major equipment purchases and budget preparation are decisions commonly made by the superintendent and possibly some supervisory staff members. However, it is important to look for ways that employees can have input in decisions that affect their work. Employee involvement can lead to improvements that management would not have implemented or even thought of on their own. Nobody knows more about how to do the job, or improve it, than the person who does it every day. Create a climate on your golf course where comments, feedback, and ideas on how to do a better job are encouraged. For example, some employers have even created bonus programs to reward employees for cost cutting or productivity suggestions that are implemented.

10. Minimize weaknesses and maximize strengths

Even the most outstanding employees have weaknesses with which they struggle. They have work that they dislike or do not feel that they do very well. Effective managers become aware of the weaknesses and patiently try to address those weaknesses with the employee slowly over a period of time. At the same time, they continue to emphasize and focus on an employee's strengths, by encouraging and praising the employee based on their strengths. Belittling or focusing unduly on weaknesses can affect self-esteem and productivity. Most managers have to work at trying not to over-focus on an employee's weaknesses.

Summary

A truly motivated golf-course staff is not something that happens by accident. It results from an increased understanding of motivational principles on the part of course superintendents and supervisors. In addition, it requires constant effort and continuing communication with employees.

Today's modern workforce is much more likely to be motivated by the motivation factors identified by Herzberg, including a feeling of personal accomplishment, achievement of increasing responsibility, a sense of importance to the organization, and involvement in decisionmaking.

It is your role as a manager to create this environment where employees will be motivated through considering the wants and needs of your employees, offering praise and encouragement, implementing an effective compensation strategy, and making employees' jobs meaningful. Those who invest the time in understanding and implementing motivational principles receive substantial rewards in the form of employee job satisfaction and productivity.

References

Arthur, D. 1987. Managing human resources in small and mid-sized companies. Amacom, New York, NY.

Blanchard, K. and S. Johnson. 1982. The one minute manager. The Berkeley Publishing Group, New York, NY.

Cohn, T. and R.A. Lindberg. 1984. Practical personnel policies for small business. Van Nostrand Reinhold Publishing, New York.

Heneman, H.G., D.P. Schwab, J.A. Fossum, and L.D. Dyer. 1986. Personnel/Human resource management. Richard D. Irwin, Homewood, IL.

How to build and keep a motivated workforce. 1985. Institute for Management, Old Saybrook, CT.

Locke, E.A. and G.P. Latham. 1984. Goal setting: A management technique that works! Prentice Hall, Englewood Cliffs, NJ.

Korvach, K.A. 1980. Why motivational theories don't work. S.A.M. Advance Management Journal. Spring.

Maas, G.G. 1990. Keep your farm employees motivated. Hoard's Dairyman. January 10.

Plunkett, W.R. 1979. Supervision: The direction of people at work. William C. Brown Company Publishers, Dubuque, IA.

Psychology today, An introduction, 2nd ed. 1972. CRM Books, Del Mar, CA.

11

The Golf Course Superintendent as a Communicator

Effective communication is critical to employee motivation and golf course productivity. The discussion on leadership in Chapter 9 included the crucial link between using task and supporting behaviors effectively to enhance employee productivity and motivation. These behaviors require a foundation of good communication in order to be effective.

Superintendents utilize communication in three ways. The first is to convey and receive information, facts, and plans. The second is to develop the desired job environment by building commitment to the course's vision, providing support and coaching, and conveying feelings and emotions. The third use is the resolution of conflicts. The first two sections of this chapter address utilizing listening and speaking to create more effective communication, while the third section focuses directly on managing conflict.

Listening

Key Points
- Allow the person talking to finish.
- Listen to hear what is being said.

Effective listening is essential to good communication. The key is to allow the person talking to finish talking before responding. Many of us naturally respond too soon in the conversation, either to defend ourselves against real or perceived attacks or to introduce our own ideas or observations.

Here is an example of how not to listen:

Employee: "I'm really upset. Mr. Jones from the Green Committee
     told me off about that problem spot on the eighth green right in
     front of two foursomes."
Superintendent: "You shouldn't be upset. He is on the Green Com-
     mittee and he's concerned about a legitimate problem."

What is the problem here? The superintendent interjected his opinion
when the employee had only begun to discuss what happened. The employee
is left feeling that the superintendent is not concerned about his or her feelings
or opinions. The employee is likely to become less open, more uncertain, and
less motivated.

Now look at a better response and see what happens:

Employee: "I'm really upset at Mr. Jones."
Superintendent: "You seem very upset. Tell me more about what
     happened."
Employee: "When explaining the problem on the eighth green to his
     friends, he was so loud that others nearby could hear. Then he
     asked me what we were doing about it."
Superintendent: "Was it what he said or the loudness that upset you?"
Employee: "Both. No, mainly the loudness. But, Mr. Jones is
     always loud."
Superintendent: "Did anything else happen?"
Employee: "No. Well, not there. I guess I'm still mad at Mr. Jones
     for his criticism at the Little League game last night."

In this version of the example, the superintendent did not seem to do a lot.
The role was one of listening and facilitating the employee talking through his
or her feelings. Note that through this facilitation, the superintendent enabled
the employee to realize that his reaction to Mr. Jones was at least partially a
result of his anger from an incident the evening before. In this version, the
employee is likely to feel there was a good discussion and the incident is
closed.

The second key is to listen carefully so you hear what is said, not what
you thought was going to be said or what you wanted to be said. In the
following dialogue a superintendent has just told her staff that one of the
employees has been injured and all maintenance staff have to work extra
hours. Bob, the employee she expects to resist the most, approaches her after
the meeting:

Bob: "I have some real concerns about this extra work. I am taking a course and have some other plans but…"

Superintendent: (interrupting) "I knew you would be a problem. But we all have to do our share. We have no choice."

Bob: "Please, let me finish. What I am trying to say is that I want to do my part. I'm even willing to do more than my share. However, it is important to me that my time be scheduled so I can finish my class and attend my sister's wedding next weekend."

Superintendent: "Oh! Oh! That's great. We can arrange that."

The outcome was positive, but the conversation was very awkward when Bob was not allowed to finish his sentence. Notice that the superintendent made an incorrect assumption about what Bob would say and did not allow him to finish speaking. Think what might have happened had Bob not persisted.

Nonverbal Communication Tactics

Key Points
- Nonverbal communication tactics are used to provide a positive setting for communication.
- Nonverbal tactics include appropriate location, eye contact, open body posture, and receptive facial expressions.

Effective listening can be enhanced by appropriate atmosphere, setting, and attitudes; these items are used to obtain the proper setting and are referred to as nonverbal communication tactics. Tactics discussed below include location, eye contact, facial expression, and body posture.

Location is particularly important, as the person talking is often your subordinate and is likely to be uneasy about the discussion. Anything that emphasizes your authority position can hinder the discussion. Examples include sitting behind a desk, standing while the speaker sits, and having the discussion in your office. Ensuring that the discussion is in a quiet, private location enhances your listening and the employee's willingness to communicate.

Establishing and maintaining eye contact with the speaker communicates your interest in what is being said. Looking up tends to indicate boredom and looking down is a sign of defensiveness (Blanchard and Tracey, 1989). How have you felt when someone you were talking to looked bored or was daydreaming?

Positioning yourself with an open body posture and facing the speaker conveys that you are interested and listening. Sitting or standing with your arms folded indicates that both your body and your mind are closed. How do you feel when you talk to someone whose body is facing to the side even if their head is turned to face you? It is hard to be certain they are really interested and paying attention.

Facial expressions are one of the purest forms of communication. When you nod agreement or at least acknowledge understanding, you are confirming that you are listening. On the other hand, you can negate everything discussed in this section with one frown or a sigh of disgust or disapproval.

The tactics in this section can be effectively used to improve communication only when you are committed to improved listening and when you are sincerely interested in what the other person is saying. They appear artificial when used to hide poor listening skills or lack of interest.

Active Listening

Key Points
- Active listening is used to assist others in solving their own problems
- Active listening creates an environment for open communication and employee development.

The listener is now taking "active" responsibility for understanding both the content of and feelings behind what is being said. Gordon (1970) describes active listening as a communication skill the listener can use to help others solve their own problems.

Now look at an example. An employee approaches you and says, "The deadline to finish fertilizing the fairways is not realistic." The usual response would be to insist that the deadline is realistic. An active listening response, however, could be, "It sounds like you are concerned about whether you can meet the deadline." The advantage of this response is twofold. First, you show empathy for the employee's position. Second, you can now talk about both the employee's feelings and the practical issue of meeting the deadline.

An open communication climate is created through active listening. The listener better understands what a person means and how the person feels about situations and problems. Active listening is a skill that communicates acceptance and increases interpersonal trust between employees and their supervisor. It also facilitates problem solving.

Active listening should not be used to manipulate people to behave or think the way others think they should. The listener also should not "parrot" a message by repeating the exact words. Empathy is a necessary ingredient—the listener should communicate some emotion toward the sender's message. Active listening is not appropriate when there is no time to deal with the situation or when someone is asking only for factual information. Also, it is important that the listener be sensitive to nonverbal messages about the right time to stop giving feedback. For example, if an employee begins to look at the clock or door, shift restlessly, or fold his or her arms, the employee is ready to end the conversation. Avoiding these common pitfalls makes active listening a more effective communication skill and increases the productivity of your golf course maintenance staff.

Speaking

Effective communication through speaking requires use of the nonverbal tactics previously discussed to ensure that listener and speaker have the best possible environment. In addition, verbal tactics can be used to better enable the listener to hear the intended message. In this section we consider three verbal tactics—questioning, prompting, clarifying—and a communication tool: "I statements."

Questioning

Key Points
- Questioning enables the superintendent to involve the staff in problem solving.
- Open-ended questioning keeps communication going.

Golf course superintendents are continually working with employees to accomplish golf course tasks and goals. Asking questions is an effective communication tool to assist maintenance staff in problem solving. Questioning is used to encourage employees and others to continue talking. Questions can be open-ended or closed-ended. The following examples illustrate the difference:

Closed: "Did you talk to the golf pro about his complaint regarding the eighth green?"
Open: "How did you resolve the golf pro's complaint about the eighth green?"

Closed: "Did you have any trouble with the mower today?"
Open: "How did the mower operate today?"

Closed: "Are you going to arrive for work on time?"
Open: "What are you going to do to ensure you arrive at work on time?"

Open-ended questions are used to keep communication going so you can gather additional information. These questions begin with "Tell me about," "Describe for me," "How," or "What." Closed-ended questions are used to get specific information and to gain or regain control of a conversation. These questions begin with "When," "Who," "Did you," or "Where" (The Core Corporation, 1988).

Prompting

Key Points
- Prompting is another way to encourage employees to continue talking.
- Tactics include encouraging prods, calling by name and using an even tone of voice.

Employees are often reluctant to speak openly with their supervisor and are often uncertain when they feel they must speak with their supervisor. As a supervisor, the golf course superintendent can encourage a reluctant communicator by using supportive prods when they appear to have stopped talking. Interjections include "Go on," "I see," "I understand," "Yes, go ahead," and "uh-huh." Calling the person by their name shows personal interest and can refocus the attention of the speaker. An even tone of voice, with no yelling or soft voice, increases the chance of being heard and encourages a reluctant communication partner.

In the following dialogue, a new, nervous employee, George, is expressing his concern about his assigned task of digging a hole for a new tree. Playing baseball the previous evening, he sprained his ankle.

> George: "I don't think I should shovel dirt today. No, I'll try it."
> Superintendent: "George, what is it? Is there a problem?" *(calling by name)*
> George: "Well, it's my ankle. I hurt it."
> Superintendent: "I see, tell me more." *(encouraging prods)*
> George: "I hurt it playing baseball last night and shoveling could injure it more. Not to mention, it will hurt even more."
> Superintendent: "I understand. You can switch jobs with Rich. George, you should feel free to talk to me at any time." *(calling by name)*

Assuming the superintendent used an even tone of voice, all three prompting tactics were utilized in this dialogue.

Clarifying

Key Points
- Clarifying is used to ensure that the listener understands what is said.
- Tactics include echo/restating, active paraphrasing/repeating, and summarizing.

While questioning and prompting are used to encourage conversation, clarifying is used primarily to make certain the listener understands what is being said. After the listening skills discussed in the previous section are used, the superintendent uses clarifying statements to show he or she has heard and understood.

Consider the following dialogue between Susan and her superintendent:

Susan: "We have a problem on the 13th hole. The green speed is only six feet."

Superintendent: "You said the green speed on the 13th hole is only six feet?" *(echo/restating)*

Susan: "The green is really soggy, especially on the side next to that new sand bunker. I think a drainage problem has been created by building the bunker."

Superintendent: "You're telling me that the excavation for that new bunker may be diverting water onto the green." *(active paraphrasing/repeating)*

Susan: "Yes. I spent almost an hour trying to figure out exactly what was diverting the water, but I'm not certain. I think we need to call the contractor who did the work on the bunker."

Superintendent: "Let's see if I understand. The green speed problem is caused by changes in drainage caused by construction of the new sand bunker. You think we should contact the contractor to investigate the problem." *(summarizing)*

Note that in the first comment *echo/restating* was used to repeat exactly what was said to make certain the details were understood correctly. *Active paraphrasing* was used so the superintendent was certain he understood what Susan was saying. Summarizing was used to provide one last chance to make certain everything Susan said was understood.

Summarizing can also be effective when a discussion seems unclear or out of control and needs to get back on track. As the listener, summarizing the speaker's points can help them refocus on the important information.

"I" Statements

Key Points
- Focus on specific actions of employees.
- Recognize that feelings are very personal.

We frequently hear statements like "You made me mad!" or "You upset me." Statements of this type do not contribute to effective communication for two reasons. First, it is not the person that "makes me mad" or "upsets me." It is a specific act. Blaming the person rather than focusing on the specific act hinders effective communication. Second, "mad" and "upset" are feelings, and feelings are very personal. A more effective way of communicating the same message is with an "I" statement.

As an example, suppose the "you upset me" resulted from Wayne being late for work. An "I" statement for this situation would be, "Wayne, when you are continually late to work, I feel upset. I want you to be on time." The form of an "I" statement is:

1. State the facts.   "When......, this happens."
2. State your feelings.   "I feel..."
3. State what you want.   "I want..."

"I" statements are feeling messages. By disclosing your personal perceptions and feelings in a nonthreatening, nonaggressive way, open communication is facilitated. In order to effectively discuss interpersonal issues, you need to share your perceptions, feelings, and needs. "I" statements are helpful because they create empathy, build trust, and facilitate understanding. Figure 11.1 displays the use of "I" statements in several situations.

Managing Conflict on the Golf Course

Key Points
- Conflict can be either good or bad.
- Resolution of conflict should be the focus.
- Conflict is the source of all change.

Conflict is a daily reality for everyone. Whether at home or at work, an individual's needs, goals, objectives, and values invariably come into opposition with those of other people. Some conflicts are relatively minor and easy to handle. However, conflicts of greater magnitude require a strategy for successful resolution to prevent them from creating constant tension.

Consider the following conflict situations:

1. As the superintendent is presenting the fertilization plan for the golf season, Laura objects, arguing for a new recommendation that she learned at a fertilization class she has just completed. At first the superintendent is defensive, but then he remembers that one objective of this golf course is to ensure that all practices are

Figure 11.1. Examples of "I" Statements

Situation:	"I" statement:
You are proud of the accomplishments your staff has produced working as a team.	"When we accomplish so much as a team, I feel very proud. I want us to continue to work effectively as a team."
Situation: You are disappointed and frustrated that an employee can not remember simple instructions.	**"I" statement:** "When what I think are simple instructions are not followed, I feel disappointed and frustrated. I want you to listen more carefully, write things down if necessary and ask questions if anything is not clear."
Situation: You are disappointed but happy that your assistant superintendent was not offered the superintendent's job she had applied for.	**"I" statement:** "I am disappointed you weren't offered the job but happy you will remain here. I want you to continue your excellent work with this course."

completely up-to-date. The outcome of this exchange is that the staff works together to adjust the fertilization plans to include the latest recommendation.

2. Two employees have arguments nearly every week when work schedules are posted. They look at each other's schedules and complain that the other has better times. Each week the superintendent says, "Don't argue. We're a team here, so don't disagree." Now all of the staff are complaining about work schedules; morale and productivity are dropping.

Three points can be made by contrasting these two situations. First, conflict is not good or bad; it can be either. Figure 11.2 outlines good and bad consequences of conflict. The second point is not whether conflict is present—for it will be present in any relationship—but that it must be resolved. Conflict is present in both situations, but only in the first does the superintendent manage to resolve the conflict. The third point, as illustrated in the first situation, is that conflict is the source of all change.

Managing conflict is addressed by focusing on three topics. The first is to further understand conflict by defining the conflict cycle. Alternative conflict management styles are described in the second section. Using these styles and other tactics in conflict resolution is the topic of the third section.

Figure 11.2. Pros and Cons of Conflict

Good Side of Conflict	Bad Side of Conflict
• Properly managed, conflict can be beneficial. • Conflict is the root of change. • People learn and grow as a result of conflict. • Conflict stimulates curiosity and imagination. • Conflict helps to relieve monotony and boredom. • Conflict can provide diagnostic information about problem areas. • After conflict, closer unity may be reestablished.	• Prolonged conflict can create stress and be injurious to your physical and mental health. • Conflict diverts time, energy, and money away from reaching important goals. • Conflict often results in self interest at the expense of the organization. • Intensive conflict may result in lies and distorted information.

Understanding Conflict

Key Points
- The conflict cycle includes issues, triggering events, conflict behavior, and consequences.
- Positive outcomes of conflict produce good feelings (eustress); unsatisfactory outcomes produce bad feelings (distress).

Conflict occurs whenever the concerns of two people appear to be incompatible. As a process, conflict begins when one party in an interaction perceives that another has prevented his/her needs from being met. Conflict is a cyclical process. Overt conflict usually occurs only periodically when people's contrary values or goals surface through a triggering event. The underlying issues lie dormant until something happens to trigger conflict

Figure 11.3. The Cycle of Conflict

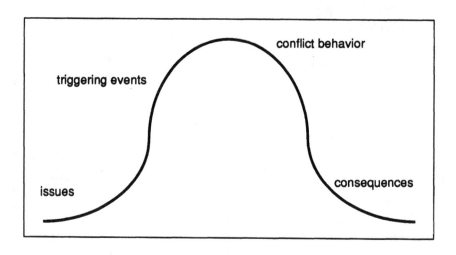

behavior. Once triggered, the conflict usually becomes less pronounced over time, and the issues may not be apparent until the next triggering event causes the cycle to repeat itself. The four elements—issues, triggering events, conflict behavior, and consequences—are identified in Figure 11.3 (Walton 1987).

Most conflict cycles are not static. Without conflict resolution, conflict cycles usually escalate, either in frequency, intensity, or both. Most conflicts are resolved by deescalation of the cycle. Rarely is resolution so successful and complete that the next triggering event has no impact on the behavior of the parties to the conflict. Try to identify the conflict cycle elements the next time you are enmeshed in a conflict situation. The four elements are illustrated by a sample conflict situation in Figure 11.4.

Conflict always produces stress. Stress is the response of the body to demands made upon it. Stress is not bad; in fact, stress is necessary for us to perform in life. The outcome of stress is what is critical.

Positive outcomes produce eustress, with good after-feelings. In situation #1, there was stress when Laura objected to the fertilization plan; however, everyone felt good about the outcome, producing eustress. The second situation produces distress, or bad after-feelings, because the issue is not being resolved. The following sections provide the superintendent with skills to resolve conflicts, producing more eustress, fewer suspicions, and less distrust, and greater golf course productivity.

Figure 11.4. Conflict Cycle Analysis

The following illustrates the four elements of the conflict cycle using Situation #2, in the introduction to conflict.

Issue: The two employees are not satisfied with their work schedules and each believes that the other is getting preferential treatment. There may well be interpersonal differences as well.

Triggering Event: The weekly posting of the work schedules.

Behavior: Employees argue with each other and complain to the superintendent.

Consequences: Other employees are upset and begin complaining. Motivation and productivity of all employees decreases.

Notes: 1. Not all triggering events occur this regularly.
2. As here, the consequences can reach far beyond the issue itself.
3. This conflict appears to be escalating.

Conflict Management Styles

Key Points
- The styles are competing, collaborating, accommodating, avoiding, and compromising.
- The styles serve as alternative "tools" for the superintendent to use to resolve conflict.

Just as different seedbeds require different varietal mixtures and different leadership situations call for different leadership styles, specific conflict situations are best resolved with different conflict management styles. Knowledge of the styles provides the superintendent with tools to use to resolve conflict situations. Five styles are identified (Ross, 1982):

Competing

The competing style is used to meet one's own needs and concerns at the expense of other parties. It is the most assertive and least cooperative style. To achieve the desired outcome, the competitor uses whatever power is available and acceptable, e.g., position or rank, information, expertise, persuasive ability, or coercion.

Collaborating

Collaborating involves the maximum use of both cooperation and assertiveness. A collaborative style is used when attempting to satisfy the needs and concerns of both parties. Collaboration requires more commitment than the other styles, and usually takes more time and energy. Collaboration is also the best style to use when it is essential that the parties involved in a conflict situation be committed to the agreed upon solution.

Accommodating

The accommodating style is characterized by cooperative and unassertive behavior. Accommodation means placing the other party's needs and concerns above one's own. Those who use accommodation to excess may feel resentful that their own ideas, needs and concerns are not receiving the attention they deserve.

Avoiding

The avoiding style is characterized by both uncooperative and unassertive behavior. Those employing this style simply do not address the conflict and are indifferent to others' needs and concerns. They evade the issue, withdraw from the discussion, or may not even be present for the resolution.

Compromising

The compromising style is used to find a solution to the conflict when collaboration fails. The intent of this style is to find a solution that partially fulfills the concern of all parties to the conflict.

Figure 11.5 contains a comparison of the five conflict management styles based on the emphasis on one's own needs and others' needs and on the desired outcome in terms of who wins and loses in the conflict. One might conclude from viewing the table that the collaborating style is always the best. That conclusion is not correct because a win-win solution is not always

Figure 11.5. Comparison of Conflict Management Styles

	Emphasis on own needs	Emphasis on others' needs	Desired outcome (self-other)
Competing	yes	no	win-lose
Collaborating	yes	yes	win-win
Accommodating	no	yes	lose-win
Avoiding	no	no	lose-lose
Compromising	some	some	win and lose

possible, nor is the time always available to find such a solution. The competing style is necessary when the conflict must be resolved with your solution. Golf course examples where the competing style could be appropriate include any situation where safety is threatened, circumstances involving service to the golfer, and any conflict where the wrong outcome could negatively impact the future of the golf course.

Accommodating and avoiding, the unassertive styles, also have potential uses by golf course superintendents. Accommodating can be utilized to help build confidence and rapport with the employee or colleague with whom you are having a conflict. It is possible that the superintendent in conflict situation #1 was accommodating to Laura to increase her confidence and to illustrate the value of training. The avoiding style can be effectively utilized in situations that are not worth your time or to diffuse explosive situations by postponing them to a later time when resolution is more likely.

Conflict Resolution

Conflict resolution is a difficult but important responsibility of the superintendent. The understanding of conflict and the conflict styles can be best used when you utilize a well-designed conflict resolution process. The following is an eight-step process:

1. Analyze the conflict situation and develop a conflict resolution plan, including choosing the most appropriate conflict management style or styles.
2. Explain the situation the way you see it. Emphasize that you are presenting your perception of the problem. Give specific facts and feelings when possible.
3. Describe how the conflict is affecting performance. Focus attention on the work-related problem and away from the per-

sonalities of people involved. Present the problem in a way that is readily understood, and concentrate on important issues.

4. Ask for other viewpoints to be explained. Before proposing solutions, gather as much information as possible. This step confirms that you respect the other person's opinion and need his or her cooperation. Listen carefully while he or she talks and be open to learning and changing. Use the communication skills and tactics discussed in this chapter.

5. Agree on the problem. Summarize the various viewpoints and state clearly the problem that you and the other participant(s) think needs to be solved. Once both parties agree on the problem, everyone can more easily focus on developing solutions.

6. Explore and discuss possible solutions. In order to ensure shared ownership of the problem's resolution, all participants in the conflict should be involved in developing solutions. The synergy developed may result in better solutions than any participant would have produced alone.

7. Agree on each person's role in solving the problem. Every person involved must clearly understand his or her role in the solution and accept responsibility as an individual and team member for making it work.

8. Set a date for follow-up. A follow-up meeting allows you to evaluate progress and make adjustments as necessary. People are much more likely to follow through when they know they are held accountable for their commitments at a follow-up meeting.

Figure 11.6 contains twelve suggestions for improving communication and more effectively resolving conflict.

A Final Note

An effective communicator is assertive and sensitive without being aggressive. Sensitive means taking the time to clearly understand another person's positions and feelings and respecting those positions and feelings—in a word, having empathy for others. Assertive means clearly and calmly presenting one's own positions and feelings.

Aggressiveness should be minimized, as it is very destructive to good communication, especially when you already have an authority position. Subordinates are easily intimidated by any show of aggressiveness by their supervisor. Being assertive without being aggressive requires effective use of the communication skills and tactics presented in this chapter.

Figure 11.6.

Communication Suggestions for Successful Conflict Resolution
1. Focus on conquering the problem, not one another.
2. Involve everyone in the process to create a sense of shared responsibility for the solution.
3. Evaluate solutions in terms of quality and acceptance to the parties.
4 Ask questions to elicit information, not to belittle the other party.
5. Provide feedback that is descriptive, specific, and nonjudgmental.
6. Ensure that power is equal or that differences in power are ignored.
7. Share information equally.
8. Believe that mutually acceptable solutions are possible and desirable.
9. Trust each other.
10. Eliminate defensiveness and anger.
11. Jointly define the problem.
12. Separate the problem description, solution generation, and solution evaluation phases of the discussion.

Summary

Communication skills are crucial to your ability to lead and encourage the golf course maintenance staff. Communication is typically used by golf course supervisors in three ways: (1) to convey and receive information, (2) to develop an encouraging work environment through coaching and developing a vision, and (3) for the resolution of conflict. In order to increase the information flow at your golf course and develop an effective work environment, you should utilize several tactics of effective communication.

First, you should develop your listening skills. We all know how to hear, but listening requires practice. When listening to an employee, let them finish speaking, and really listen to hear what they are actually saying, not what you think or want them to say. Additionally, nonverbal communication tactics such as body posture and facial expressions can really help to create a more positive communication interaction. "Active" listening is another effective skill that you should utilize in your supervisory role. The goal of active listening is to enable others to solve their own problems, and show empathy and concern for others' feelings.

Communication involves not only listening, but also speaking. The verbal tactics of questioning, prompting, and clarifying all aim to improve communication interactions by encouraging conversation. Each of these tactics helps you to better understand what is being said to you, and enables you to show support to your employees. "I" statements are an effective way to discuss disruptive behaviors or an uncomfortable situation in a nonthreatening, nonaggressive way. "I" statements place the focus on the feelings created by a specific behavior, not by the person. By using "I" statements, you can create an environment of trust and facilitate understanding.

Managing conflict is the third function of supervisory communication. Remember, the focus is not on eliminating conflict from your golf course. Conflict will always be present, and it does have positive consequences. Your focus should be on minimizing the negative conflict situations, and resolving conflict situations to the maximum benefit of all involved. Study the various conflict styles presented in this chapter, and use the appropriate style for the specific conflict situation you are faced with.

Most of all, have empathy for others, and present yourself in an assertive but not aggressive manner. By utilizing effective listening, speaking, and conflict resolution tactics, the communication at your golf course should improve, and you will set a positive example for your subordinates.

References

Blanchard, K. and B. Tracey. 1989. Blanchard and Tracey on leadership. Blanchard Training and Development, Escondido, CA.

The Core Corporation. 1988. Performance skills in effective store management: Trainer's guide. Food Marketing Institute.

Fisher, R., W. Ury, and B. Patton. 1991. Getting to yes: Negotiating agreement without giving in. Penguin Books, New York.

Gordon, T. 1970. Parent effectiveness training. Peter H. Wyden, New York.

Ross, M.B. 1982. In The 1982 annual for facilitators, trainers, and consultants. University Associates, San Diego, CA.

Thomas, K.W. 1976. Conflict and conflict management. In M.D. Dunnette (Ed.). Handbook of industrial and organization psychology (Vol. II). Rand McNally, Chicago, IL.

Walton, R.E. 1987. Managing conflict: Interpersonal dialogue and third-party roles. Addison-Wesley, Reading, MA.

12

Employee Discipline and Discharge

The theme of this book has been to attract and retain the most qualified individuals for golf course maintenance positions and to encourage peak performance through leadership, motivation, and participatory management. In short, we have encouraged performance and productivity by treating the people on the golf course maintenance staff as the most important resource of the golf course. Yet, an inevitable fact of life for any manager is that sometimes it will be necessary to discipline an employee and occasionally it will even be necessary to terminate employment. Discipline and discharge policies are in the best interests of both the employer and the employee because they correct improper or inadequate performance and restore a positive work environment. To be effective, the issues of discipline and discharge must be considered and addressed in a professional manner, well before they are needed.

As we consider employee discipline and discharge, we should think back to the reason why the golf course staff exists. The golf course exists for the enjoyment of its customers: the paying public or the members. To maximize the recreational enjoyment of those individuals, the golf course must be maintained in a professional manner. Top performance is required from all staff members. To attain peak productivity, the superintendent must have a vision of what an excellent golf course is, communicate that vision to the staff, create performance standards, and provide the supervision and physical resources necessary to meet those performance standards. A superintendent uses discipline when an employee's behavior is not consistent with the policies of the organization or the performance standards established for the individual.

Discipline benefits individual employees by helping to put them back on the right track toward expected job performance. Through the use of disciplinary procedures, the effective manager corrects employees' job performance to ensure their livelihood and their quality of life. Often constructive criticism and successful problem resolution restore their self esteem and productivity.

Discharge can also be viewed in a positive light. The employee is hired to help the organization meet its goals and objectives. At the point when the employee is no longer making a positive contribution, discharge may be the only alternative. If the employee does not have the skills or desire to help the organization meet its goals and objectives, it is in the best interest of both parties to terminate employment. Discharge, however, should be viewed as a last resort, after the discipline procedures outlined in this chapter have been carefully followed.

A thorough understanding of discipline and discharge issues is critical to the superintendent for two important reasons. First, both discipline and discharge are emotionally charged issues. It is rare to find a manager who does not feel uncomfortable when faced with a discipline or discharge situation. Because of the emotional nature of these issues, it is often natural to procrastinate or avoid addressing them quickly and directly. Avoiding an obvious discipline or discharge situation is a mistake. It has a negative impact on the organization's performance, creates stress for the other staff members, and often aggravates the situation. The second reason discipline and discharge issues are so critical is that legal problems can result for the golf course and the superintendent if they are not handled properly. Common legal pitfalls can be avoided by following a set of practical procedures for addressing discipline and discharge. This chapter presents the steps that should be used when discipline and discharge situations arise with the golf course maintenance staff.

Employee Discipline

The occurrence of problems requiring disciplinary action is influenced by most of the topics discussed in this book. A manager's abilities to effectively recruit, hire, train, motivate, provide appropriate leadership for, and effectively communicate with productive people all affect how successful an employee is in the job. Perhaps the topic most closely related to the issues of discipline and discharge is performance management, covered in Chapter 7. Performance management practices include goal setting, coaching, feedback, and evaluation of employee job performance. The coaching and feedback component of performance management relates directly to discipline issues. Coaching and feedback provided on a daily basis allow an employee's immediate supervisor to monitor performance, compliment and recognize good performance, discuss tasks that are not performed properly, and emphasize areas that need attention to ensure peak employee performance and achievement of the golf course's goals. However, there is a point at which ongoing coaching and feedback are no longer appropriate for some forms of employee behavior. Discipline discussions must then be initiated.

Consider the example of an employee who has been on the golf course staff for the past four summers and has always performed well. Recently the employee has begun to arrive to work late. At first it was occasionally 5 to 10 minutes, but in the last three weeks, 15 to 30 minutes late three times each week has been the norm. The supervisor spoke to the employee informally about the problem twice, with no change in behavior. It is now time to move from the coaching and feedback phase of performance management to the initial phase of discipline discussions.

Most employee discipline issues can be categorized into two broad areas: violation of rules and policies, and unacceptable job performance. An employee handbook is an excellent tool for conveying the rules and policies of the organization and their importance early in the employment relationship. Rules should be written clearly and communicated to all employees. They should be reviewed periodically to ensure that they reflect the golf course's current philosophy and needs.

Obviously, there are different levels of rules violations. Some are relatively minor, others are more serious; each should be dealt with accordingly. Above all, these issues should not be ignored. While concerns like absenteeism and tardiness are relatively minor when compared to issues such as theft or drug abuse, they must not be allowed to continue; they can easily become larger performance problems.

Serious rule infractions may include:

- theft of company property
- falsification of company records or documents
- consuming alcohol or drugs on company property
- insubordination, defined as abusive behavior toward management or refusal to comply with work assignments and requests
- being absent for two days without notifying the company
- fighting or aggressive behavior toward other individuals in the workplace

Certain employee safety violations may also be included in this list (Harwell, 1985). The superintendent should initiate positive discipline procedures when rules or policy infractions are considered serious enough to warrant disciplinary action.

Unacceptable performance may also lead to disciplinary procedures. Assuming an employee has been adequately trained and has been supervised using a performance management approach, the incidence of performance problems requiring discipline should be relatively low. Discipline problems begin when an employee ignores previously stated standards of performance. Whenever performance deteriorates, it is imperative that the supervisor discuss the performance issues with the employee immediately so that it does not deteriorate further or affect the performance or morale of coworkers. Continued performance problems are then addressed with disciplinary procedures.

The Positive Discipline Approach

Key Points
The four steps in a positive discipline approach are:
- provide a **verbal** reminder
- provide a **written** reminder
- provide a **decisionmaking leave day**
- **terminate** employment

When performance difficulties reach a point where the manager feels that ongoing coaching and feedback suggested in the performance management approach are no longer working, disciplinary action should be initiated without delay. Throughout this book we have suggested an approach for managing golf course employees that includes involving employees in making decisions and empowering them to accept responsibility, exceed expectations, and work as a team for the common good of the golf course. The steps involved in pursuing positive disciplinary action are consistent with this philosophy.

Two common management philosophies used in employee discipline are (1) progressive discipline, and a more modern approach called (2) positive discipline. Both approaches are similar in that each uses a progressive sequence of steps, starting with less severe disciplinary steps and proceeding to more severe disciplinary steps if performance is not improved. The main difference is the emphasis on the employee's active participation in the process of positive discipline, which provides the employee with choices for his or her own behavior (Osigweh and Hutchison, 1989). Progressive discipline relies more on the traditional use of punishment in discipline and tends not to involve the employee other than to convey the message to "stop the unacceptable performance or be punished." The advantage of the positive discipline approach is that legal liability may be reduced because the employee becomes an active participant in the process. The following discipline approach adheres closely to a positive discipline philosophy.

Since each step is important in the process and must be undertaken carefully and properly, let's discuss the procedures for conducting each step (Osigweh and Hutchison, 1989; Brennan, 1989).

Step 1: Provide a Verbal Reminder

Key Points
- Address specific unacceptable behavior.
- Explore causes of problem and possible solutions.
- Communicate specific change expected.
- Express confidence that the problem will be solved.

This step initiates the discipline process by providing a warning over and above the ongoing coaching and feedback that the employee generally receives. When the discipline process begins, the atmosphere surrounding the interaction between the employee and his or her supervisor should change appropriately. When the supervisor provides ongoing coaching and feedback, the atmosphere is informal and supportive. In a disciplinary situation, the supervisor should create more of an air of seriousness and formality. The supervisor should provide a place where the conversation with the employee can be conducted privately and without interruption. It is important to stick to the subject at hand. For example, a superintendent who is delivering a verbal reminder may want to approach the employee working alone out on the course and have the discussion there. Many superintendents conduct important discussions in the pickup truck while traveling between job sites. This technique provides a private place for a discussion and is not likely to raise suspicions or concerns among other staff members. As the disciplinary discussions become more serious, a more formal setting like the superintendent's office may be preferable.

The supervisor conducting the verbal warning should remind the employee of the appropriate performance standards and expectations and of the employee's responsibility to meet those standards. This initial attempt at employee involvement encourages the employee to take responsibility for the improvement of his or her performance. The manager should also make it clear that his or her job is to assist and support the employee so that top performance can be achieved. It is imperative that the manager has all the details and has checked their accuracy before speaking with the employee. This initial disciplinary meeting has four parts:

- *Define the problem in terms of failure to meet previously set performance standards.*

  It is extremely important to be specific about the behavior that has been observed, as compared to the expected behavior. Vague statements about the employee's attitude or personality-related issues are confusing and threatening to the employee. They are not behavior-based and are inappropriate in the discussion. Instead of telling an employee he or she has a bad attitude toward the job, the manager must be specific about the behavior or performance that is unacceptable.

- *Ask for and listen to the employee's reasons for the unacceptable performance and ask for suggestions on how to change.*

  At this point in the meeting, it is critical for the manager to listen to the employee, to ask questions for clarification and to elicit the employee's suggestions about what has created the problem and what the alternatives are for solving the problem.

- *Communicate the specific change expected.*

  Employer and employee must agree on acceptable performance and how it is to be achieved. The success of positive discipline relies on the manager identifying the needed changes and the employee participating in the discussion and agreeing to goals for improved performance. The desired changes should be specific and measurable. The employee must be committed to the goals and the changes required to meet them.

- *Express confidence that the problem will be solved.*

  Leave the disciplinary discussion on a positive note. If the employee feels that the supervisor is genuinely confident that he or she will improve, the employee is much more likely to improve his or her behavior. If the employee senses that the supervisor does not expect successful performance changes, he or she may be less motivated to change. It is recommended that the supervisor document this first meeting in writing, but not include this in the employee's personnel file (*Instructor's Guide: Supervisory Skills for Store Managers,* 1981).

Step 2: Provide a Written Reminder

Key Points
- Meet to outline recurrent unacceptable behavior.
- Avoid threats.
- Gain employee's agreement to change.
- Document the meeting in writing.

This second discussion in the disciplinary process should be taken very seriously by both manager and employee, but the manager should avoid making threats. For this discussion, it is appropriate to meet in a more formal setting, like the superintendent's office. The following steps are recommended:

- *Outline recurrent unacceptable behavior.*

  Provide the employee with specific written documentation of the behavior that is unacceptable, as well as the performance standards which need to be met. If appropriate, provide specific dates and times that the behavior occurred. After the employee reads the documentation, discuss the issues with him or her.

- *Gain the employee's agreement to change.*

  Once again, it is important to enlist the employee's participation in making a commitment to change and in defining improved performance goals. Emphasize how both the employer and the employee benefit from the employee's acceptable job performance.

- *Document the meeting in writing.*

  Make a written statement describing the important issues discussed in the meeting. When the written statement has been reviewed, discussed, and revised, if necessary, both employer and employee should sign it, and the employee should be notified that this written reminder will go in his or her personnel file. After a certain period of time (for example, one year), the superintendent may choose to remove the written documentation from the employee's file if no future problems occur. This type of policy may be specified in the employee handbook.

Step 3: Provide Decisionmaking Leave Day

Key Points
- Suspend individual for one day with pay.
- Ask employee to decide if he/she will correct behavior or choose to leave.
- Identify precise changes that must be made.
- Document in writing.

If, after proceeding with the first two steps, the behavior continues, a third meeting with the employee is arranged. The purpose of this meeting is to indicate that performance still is not acceptable and that the problem behavior cannot continue. The employee is told that he or she is to take the next day off, with pay, for the purpose of deciding whether or not he or she wants to continue employment with the golf course, and if he or she is willing to make the changes necessary so that employment can continue. During this third meeting, the precise changes that must be made if the employee wishes to continue employment should be spelled out again in very certain terms. If the problem behavior occurs again within one year, termination is automatic.

The concept of a decisionmaking leave day is relatively new. It replaces the practice of suspending the employee for one or more days without pay as more traditional programs have done. This approach has two advantages. First, it avoids bitterness or anger on the part of the employee because they have lost one or more days of pay. Second and most important, the employee continues to be actively involved in the decisionmaking process. This approach removes the role of the supervisor from one of the disciplinarian, where the message to the employee is, "You've misbehaved; now I'm punishing you." Instead, the superintendent supports the employee as a counselor, rather than punishing the employee as a disciplinarian.

When the employee returns to work, the supervisor meets with the employee immediately. The employee informs the supervisor of his or her decision. If the worker decides to stay employed in the current position, the supervisor should again express confidence that the problem behavior will be resolved and that the employee will meet performance expectations in all areas of the job. The supervisor and the employee jointly discuss and agree upon the specific changes that must occur for the employee to remain employed. It must be clear that if the problem behavior recurs or any disciplinary situation arises in the future, the employee will be immediately terminated. This step, like the previous step, should be fully documented and placed in the employee's file. Again, it is important to note that, with a positive disciplinary approach, employees participate in the decisionmaking process and take responsibility for their own actions.

Step 4: Terminate Employment

Key Points
- Be brief.
- Give specific reasons for termination.
- Provide information on employee rights or procedures.
- Collect keys and other golf course property.

After the employee has been given every opportunity to correct the problem behavior and perform according to the requirements of the job, termination is the final step in the progressive discipline process. At this point, all facts, documentation, and carefully thought-out reasons for termination should be assembled by the superintendent or immediate supervisor. All facts and documentation must be up-to-date and accurate. If the previous steps have been carefully followed there should be two positive results. First, since the positive discipline process has given the employee an opportunity to participate actively in correcting the situation, the termination should come as no surprise to the employee.

Second, by carefully following the four steps of the positive discipline process, legal problems should be minimized. Having assembled all the facts and documented them in writing at each step in the process, the supervisor is in a strong position to justify the termination if for some reason the employee decides to take legal action.

Employee Discharge

Most managers and supervisors do all they can to avoid discharge. When it is inevitable, it is important that the superintendent or supervisor be properly prepared to avoid mistakes or repercussions from the termination.

Once it becomes clear that an employee will be discharged, it may be necessary to inform and gain the support of a number of members of the management team. For example, if an assistant golf course superintendent decides that a subordinate should be terminated, it is important to discuss that decision with the golf course superintendent to enlist understanding and support. Depending on golf course policy, it may also be important to talk to a general manager or a personnel officer.

In a large organization, a personnel officer can be an important adviser in the employee discharge process. The personnel officer is knowledgeable regarding the personnel policies of the club and is also likely to have an understanding of the legal issues involved with employee termination. Advice on club personnel policies and legal issues will help the superintendent and golf course supervisors avoid mistakes that could result in legal recourse for the organization. For example, if the club uses an employee personnel handbook that describes a specific discharge policy, that policy should be carefully followed. If the policy is not followed, the employee could have a case against the club for unlawful discharge. If the supervisor or golf course superintendent knows ahead of time that there are potential legal concerns with a particular employee termination, it is always good advice to seek the assistance of an attorney before termination takes place.

Another area that requires the superintendent's attention is the atmosphere of the work environment after the termination has taken place. The golf course superintendent or supervisor should have a plan to minimize any morale problems and ease other employees' concerns over having one of their coworkers discharged. If appropriate, the supervisor may want to meet with the employees to explain what has happened and to lay out expectations for the rest of the staff. Employees with specific concerns can be encouraged to speak with the superintendent on an individual basis. It is important that the supervisor be extremely supportive of the employees and enlist their support in maintaining a strong team. Emphasize that "there is a great deal of work to do, so let's put the situation behind us and get on with the job." It is also important to remember that the reaction of the staff may not always be negative. At times, workers will be relieved to be rid of a coworker who is undermining the efforts of the team and causing morale problems.

The following is a list of suggestions and reminders for superintendents to use as they prepare for and conduct employee terminations (Finnie and Sniffin, 1984):

- *Don't go it alone.*

Terminating the employment of a staff member affects managers in different ways. For some (especially newer and younger superintendents and supervisors), it can be an emotional and disturbing experience to terminate another person's employment. If needed, the superintendent should seek the support and encouragement of trusted superintendents or managers. Other managers with experience can identify with the situation, make suggestions, and provide encouragement if the termination process becomes difficult.

- *Select an appropriate time for termination.*

The superintendent is in the best position to determine at what point in the work week to terminate employment if the employee will be asked to leave immediately. Most managers agree that this should not be done at 5 p.m. on Friday afternoon because it gives the employee too much time to become upset and possibly overreact. Rather, it is recommended that the termination interview be done early in the work week and early in the day to give the employee time to look for a job and finalize any personnel-related paperwork with the golf course personnel director or other appropriate persons.

- *Give specific reasons for the termination.*

Summarize the reasons why the employee must leave his or her position, but make it clear that there is no longer an opportunity to discuss the issues. A decision has been made, and it is the manager's responsibility to see that the discussion focuses on the future rather than rehashing the past.

- *Provide information on employee rights and policies.*

When employment is terminated, there may be a number of practical issues that must be pursued regarding payment for accrued vacation days, receiving the last paycheck, and gathering personal belongings. Again, these issues should be covered in a clear and straightforward manner. If the golf club employs a personnel officer, it may be helpful to consult that individual before the discharge meeting.

- *Be brief.*

    The supervisor conducting the termination should have an outline
    of the information to be covered and be prepared to take only a
    few minutes. If the positive discipline steps outlined early in this
    chapter have been followed, there should no longer be a need for
    much discussion. The employee was given every opportunity to
    change the behavior and the necessary changes were not made.

- *Collect any golf course property or equipment.*

    If the employee has keys, uniforms, or any other property of the
    golf course, it should be collected at the time of discharge to
    avoid the possibility that the employee will take it. It will help if
    you can be clear about exactly what pieces of property must be
    returned.

- *Be clear about when employment will be terminated.*

    The superintendent will have to make a decision regarding
    whether or not the employee will be terminated or have more
    days to work. This is particularly important if there is likely to
    be an emotional or dramatic response to the termination. In the
    majority of the cases, immediate termination may be the best
    decision to avoid morale problems with coworkers and to min-
    imize the opportunity for any type of sabotage or damage to golf
    course property or threat to other employees.

Progressive discipline leading to discharge is a relatively new concept,
and one that requires more attention and energy of the supervisor than
previous disciplinary approaches because it fully involves the employee in the
process. However, the payoffs for using this type of approach can be substantial. It allows the employee to save face as much as possible; it minimizes
legal issues for the golf course; and this approach also, if done correctly over
a long period of time, can minimize the number of terminations and build a
high level of trust between supervisors and employees.

Legal Issues

No treatment of discipline and discharge issues would be complete
without addressing the legal ramifications of these actions. In recent years,
there has been an increase in unlawful discharge cases won by employees.

These cases set precedents for future cases. In addition, there is an increase in local and regional statutes that protect workers from being fired under certain conditions. Increasingly, employers want to know under what conditions they can legally discharge employees.

One of the most basic legal concepts that applies to employee discharge is the "at will" employment doctrine. This legal concept states that, just as an employee can voluntarily quit at any time for any reason, so can the employer terminate employment at any time for any reason. Unless there is an employment contract, employees generally work on an "at will" basis. It would seem that an employer who decides to discharge an "at will" employee would be able to do so legally. While traditionally this was true, in recent years the "at will" employment doctrine has lost strength. Courts have increasingly decided against employers when they try to use the "at will" defense in wrongful discharge cases. It should be remembered that the strength of the "at will" doctrine will vary from state to state.

It continues to be a good practice to include an "at will" employment statement in an employee handbook if one exists. For example, "Your employment is entered into voluntarily and you are free to resign at any time. Similarly, because an 'at will' relationship exists, your employment may be terminated at any time."

In addition to recent court cases favoring the employee, other issues can restrict employee termination as well. For example, if there is a union contract in place, the "at will" employment doctrine is not applicable. Also, other statutes may supersede the "at will" employment doctrine. For example, if during a termination an employer discriminated against an employee based on race, religion, or some other status protected by law, the "at will" employment doctrine would not be sufficient to protect the employer. While it is not possible in this discussion to review every court case that has resulted in a ruling of unlawful discharge of employees, legal professionals suggest the following reminders that can help to minimize the risk of unlawful termination of an employee:

- *Avoid allegations of discrimination.*

   If there is evidence that managers or supervisors have discriminated against the employee on the basis of race, religion, disability, sex, age, or other factor, legal questions could arise.

- *Treat all employees similarly in discipline and discharge cases.*

   If an employee can claim that he or she has been terminated for absenteeism, but others with similar absenteeism problems were not terminated, a legal case against the employer may emerge.

Figure 12.1

Discipline Problems and Preventions	
Problem	**How to Prevent**
Employee frequently does job improperly or incompletely.	Properly train staff members and emphasize follow-up to ensure that employees have learned all parts of the job.
Employee does not understand why discipline is needed or why he or she is being disciplined, or denies allegations.	Enter into a discussion of the problem behavior only when you have specifically defined what the problem behavior is. Have facts, dates, and specific descriptions of problem behavior. Prepare yourself, and be confident that you can clearly convey your concerns to the employee.
Employee is unaware of course policies or rules, and consequently breaks rules or behaves inappropriately.	To ensure that rules are understood, the supervisor should review rules and policies with new employees and provide an opportunity to ask questions. Rules should be included in employee handbooks or posted on a bulletin board where they are accessible to all employees.
Manager procrastinates or delays dealing with an obvious problem. Problem gets worse. Work of other employees is affected.	Address problems as soon as they arise. It is easier to address a new problem than to deal with one that has escalated into a major crisis. Be sure to speak with and coach employees on a daily basis. Set aside time routinely for this purpose.
Failure to follow up once discipline has started. Employee not held accountable.	A superintendent with many responsibilities can find that he or she is "too busy" to follow up on a problem situation. Set follow-up dates. Place them on a calendar and "to do" lists so they become a top priority.
Employee lacks basic skills to do the job and is incapable of learning them.	Extra time spent carefully recruiting and selecting employees can greatly reduce selection "mistakes." Practical skills tests or trial periods can help screen out unqualified applicants.
The discipline discussion becomes an explosive confrontation.	Be prepared with a written set of notes. Stay in control of the discussion. If the employee shouts or becomes angry, avoid being drawn into a shouting match. Anticipate confrontations and involve another supervisor in the meeting, if appropriate, for support and assistance.

* *Document unacceptable performance.*

  Most of this chapter has emphasized a step-by-step approach to dealing with employee problems, including the employee's own involvement in helping to solve the problem, as well as careful documentation of unacceptable performance. Careful documentation of problems and discipline procedures will help to create a strong case for the employer if problems arise.

* *Make sure that all actions taken by management are consistent with the golf course's personnel policies.*

  If termination or discipline policies that are clearly stated in an employee policy handbook are enforced inconsistently or not adhered to in the discipline and discharge process, the employee may have a legal recourse against the employer.

The discipline and discharge discussion in this chapter is not intended to be an all-inclusive treatment of the legalities of disciplining or discharging workers. If at any point during the discipline and discharge process the superintendent or a golf course supervisor suspects potential legal difficulties, the personnel officer and/or the course attorney or other capable labor law attorney should be consulted.

Common Discipline and Discharge Problems and How To Prevent Them

Most managers and supervisors at some time in their careers have mishandled an employee discipline or discharge situation or the events leading up to one. Managers should make it a goal to reduce discipline and discharge situations to a minimum, utilizing the human resource management practices and policies that will avoid major problems early. Many of these issues have been addressed in other chapters of this book. Figure 12.1 lists common problems or, in some cases, symptoms of problems related to discipline and discharge, and suggests strategies for avoiding them.

Summary

Employee discipline and discharge are serious and emotional issues. Effective employee supervision requires continual monitoring of performance and immediate corrections to ensure peak performance. This chapter provides a series of steps that a supervisor can use to carry out discipline and discharge procedures positively and effectively. As an employee continues to behave in an unacceptable manner, the discipline procedure should move from a simple reprimand to more serious discussions. The employee should be involved in each step of the process and be expected to take responsibility for his or her actions.

The steps outlined here should be used as guidelines and suggestions. Adapt them to your specific situation and management style to be most effective. Experience has shown that managers who have developed fair, consistent, and effective discipline and discharge procedures have organizations that run smoothly, and they avoid having to discipline or discharge employees as often.

References

Allen, J.G. (Ed.). 1986. The employee termination handbook. John Wiley & Sons, NY.

Anonymous. 1981. Instructor's Guide: Supervisory skills for store managers. Food Management and Marketing Institute, Washington, D.C.

Anonymous. 1991. Employee termination manual for managers and supervisors. Commerce Clearing House, Chicago, IL.

Brennan, E.J. 1989. Performance management workbook. Prentice Hall, Englewood Cliffs, NJ.

Caskey, C.C. 1991. Constructive discipline. Supervision, October, 11–17.

Finnie, R.A. and P.B. Sniffin. 1984. Good endings: managing employee terminations. College and University Personnel Association, Washington, D.C.

Harwell, E.M. 1985. The complete manager. Chain Store Publishing Corporation, NY.

Holley, W.H., Jr. and R.S. Wolters. 1987. Employment at will: an emerging issue for small businesses. Journal of Small Business Management. October: 1–8.

Leatherwood, M.L. and L.C. Spector. 1991. Enforcements, inducements, expected utility and employee misconduct. Journal of Management 17(3):553–569.

Meyer, D.W. 1990. Right approach to avoiding wrongful discharge. Risk Management. September: 56–62.

Margerison, C. and B. Smith. 1989. The right to fire. Management decision 27(2):79–80.

Osigweh, C.A.B. and W.R. Hutchison. 1989. Positive discipline. Human Resource Management 28(3):367–383.

Sacks, S.M. 1991. The employee rights handbook. Facts on File, NY.

Spragins, E.E. 1992. How to fire. Inc. May: 66–72.

Sweet, D.H. 1989. A manager's guide to conducting terminations. Lexington Books, Lexington, MA.

Total Quality in
Golf Course Management

In our daily lives, we are surrounded by inferences that work is bad: advertisements for the lottery promise instant wealth without the necessity of work; radio disc jockeys focus on the upcoming weekend; jokes about nasty supervisors and lazy employees are commonplace. We also know individuals who love their work; many who win the lottery continue working, or later wish they had. What is the difference between those who love their jobs and those who view work as a necessary evil? One difference is the characteristics and attitudes the employees bring to the job. A second is the characteristics of the job situation. Golf course superintendents whose employees dislike their jobs usually believe it is the employee characteristics. Superintendents, like Jim Lewis at the Successful Valley Country Club, whose employees enjoy their jobs, know that supervisors have a tremendous impact on the job satisfaction of their employees.

This difference is important to employers, employees, and golfers. It is the responsibility of the golf course superintendent to maintain the golf course in a condition that meets or exceeds the golfers' expectations. As production practices and technology become more complex and golfers' expectations increase, the golf course superintendent cannot produce the highest quality golf course without a committed staff, a staff that "likes their jobs."

Workplace Trends

There are four trends that are dramatically impacting today's workplace. We live in a world that is experiencing unprecedented changes in demographics, environmental issues, health issues, and political transformations. These important societal changes affect everyone. The trends most impacting employer-employee relationships occupy less attention in the popular press, but they are at least as important. The four trends are quality, technology, changing workforce expectations, and competitiveness.

Quality

References to quality permeate today's society: advertisements, the evening news, and management seminars. Superior quality is now viewed as an essential for business success. Total quality management is a relatively new management philosophy being adopted by businesses nationwide. In a total quality management environment, quality is defined as providing the product or service that the customer wants. The objective of a customer-oriented company then is to provide a quality product or service to the customer.

Quality examples abound in the marketplace today. Ben & Jerry's ice cream is often cited as an example of a company providing quality; its growth has been spectacular. At the other extreme, IBM has struggled because it fell into the trap of believing it knew what the customer needed in computers instead of listening to the customer's demands for computer products that are easy to use.

To provide golf course quality, the superintendent must understand why people play golf. According to data compiled by the National Golf Foundation, golfers play for many reasons (Figure 13.1). The reasons are clearly oriented to recreation (78% recreational enjoyment), companionship (63% friends play), relaxation (59%), exercise (56%) and to get outdoors (54%). Data show that 42% play for the challenge, but only 27% play for the competition. Most people play golf for recreation and enjoyment. The enjoyment of the game of golf comes from enjoying the company of others, enjoying the surroundings, and enjoying the game itself. By providing the best playing conditions possible, the golf course superintendent and his/her staff add to the quality of the game for each golfer.

Technology

Technological advances are creating more and more jobs requiring intelligence, the ability to think and make decisions, and sophisticated job skills. Just look at what the advent of word processing has done to the job of a secretary. To effectively and efficiently make maximal use of a word processor requires much more skill and sophistication than a typewriter. Unfortunately, in many organizations secretaries use a computer as a glorified typewriter, resulting in a loss of productivity.

Figure 13.1.

Reasons for Currently Playing Golf	
Recreational enjoyment	78%
Friends play	63%
Relaxation	59%
Exercise	56%
Get outdoors	54%
For the challenge	42%
Relatives play	35%
Competition	27%
For the image	16%
Meet people	15%
Business reasons	12%

Source: Golf Consumer Profile, Table A.1.   Published by National Golf Foundation. 1989.

The Changing Workforce

The most important change in how individuals approach their work is their expectations of the job. As people become more educated, they are no longer looking for "a job." They are looking for a position that brings them personal satisfaction as well as adequate compensation.   Brian Tracey (Tracey, 1986) argues that anyone not committed to and excited about his or her current job should immediately seek alternative employment.

The compensation package alone is not sufficient for employees to "like their jobs." Liking the job results from satisfaction with the job tasks and the job environment. Golf course employees gain satisfaction from their job when:

1.   They participate in at least some of the decisionmaking.
2.   They feel they are accepted as part of the team.
3.   They are contributing to the success of the golf course.
4.   They are growing and developing in their ability to contribute to this or any other golf course.
5.   They find meaning in what they are doing.

Increasingly, job applicants will be looking for a job that brings them personal satisfaction as well as adequate compensation.   Ken Blanchard (Blanchard and Tracey, 1989) talks about the Fabulous Five Hundred. Instead of the 500 largest corporations, like the Fortune 500, Blanchard's list would contain 500 companies that best meet the needs of their employees and their customers. Perhaps the GCSAA should compile the Fabulous 500 golf courses.

Competitiveness

The key word in business is competitiveness. Never before has so much been known about production and management of products and services. This provides tremendous opportunities to succeed, but also ever-present opportunities to fail. The trend is for more golf courses, improved course design, and an increase in technology to improve playing conditions. An increase in the number of golf courses means greater competition among golf clubs.

The Golf Course Superintendent's Perspective

While the employee's focus is on compensation and job satisfaction, the golf course superintendent, as supervisor and employer, is focused on golf course maintenance and the needs of the golfer. Must these two perspectives be in conflict? The answer is "no." The application of modern human resource management principles, as explained in this book, is producing a virtual revolution in the relationships between employees and their employer. The seed for this revolution was the introduction of total quality management (TQM) by Dr. W. Edwards Deming more than fifty years ago. Its germination was in Japan after World War II. Its spread in the United States is being furthered first by the increased competitiveness of Japanese companies and now by many U.S. companies successfully implementing modern leadership, management, and personnel policies based on TQM principles.

Employee and employer perspectives are not in conflict, because only committed employees can successfully produce the quality required by customers while maintaining business competitiveness. Successful application of modern human resource management approaches is exciting because of the potential gain for everyone. Employers receive high productivity and superior quality; employees receive job satisfaction. Successful implementation, however, requires that the role of the golf course superintendent change dramatically. Instead of being a "boss," the golf course superintendent becomes a teacher, a coach, a supporter, and a leader. The superintendent must then view his or her role as providing employees everything they need to meet or exceed performance expectations.

The stark contrast of this win-win commitment-oriented approach with the traditional control-oriented approach is summarized in Figure 13.2. The

Figure 13.2. Management Styles: Control vs. Commitment

	Traditional Control-Oriented	**Deming Revolution Commitment-Oriented**
Employee Roles	Take orders	Ask Questions
	Do your job	Critical part of a system
Mechanism for Achievement	Do the job "right"	Exceed expectation
Emphasis	Means/tasks	Ends/accomplishments
Development of people	Managers responsible for improvement	Everyone responsible for changes
	Little need for training	Training essential for continued success
Biggest fear	Upsetting the boss	Not meeting performance expectations
Structure	Bureaucratic	Flat
	Inherently adversarial	Inherently team collegial
Employees' response	Demotivating	Motivating
Productivity	Average at best	Outstanding when successful

change from control to commitment is necessary to attain win-win outcomes because employees do not respond positively to being controlled. Rather, they resent it, and productivity suffers.

Commitment-oriented management is only successful when the golf course superintendent meets two challenges. The first is learning the principles explained in this book. The second, but more important, and often more difficult, is the acceptance and internalization of the attitudes necessary to implement these modern management principles. This acceptance has three dimensions:

1. A commitment to success.
2. An acceptance of people as the most important asset of the golf course.
3. A commitment to providing supporting behavior.

Each is discussed individually.

A Commitment to Success

Few generals have won battles when their speech to the troops was, "I'm not sure what will happen, but let's all go out and do our best." Similarly, few corporations have succeeded when the CEO had little commitment to individual or business success. Integral to your ability to develop and lead a staff of committed, satisfied individuals is your personal commitment to success.

Brian Tracey (1986) discusses 10 principles for personal success: purpose, excellence, responsibility, service, concentration, cooperation, creativity, self-development, integrity, and courage. Although all are important, the first three merit specific attention.

Tracey feels that purpose is so important that he suggests writing and then rewriting your personal purpose each day for thirty days. This purpose becomes the basis for setting specific goals and prioritizing tasks. Without clearly identified purpose, goals, and priorities, your potential to develop a committed and satisfied staff is severely reduced.

Tracey states, "True success comes only when you commit to excellence in whatever you do." Excellence means going beyond what is expected. It comes from working beyond the required eight hours per day. Success in exceeding the golfers' expectations begins with your personal commitment to excellence.

Tracey argues that complete acceptance of personal responsibility greatly enhances effectiveness by reducing or eliminating anger, denial, and stress. It also enhances the manager's ability to listen and communicate. This acceptance greatly enhances the superintendent's effectiveness in interacting with staff members. The first ingredient to a committed, winning team is your personal commitment to success. This commitment provides an example and an atmosphere in which modern management principles can thrive.

People Are the Most Important Asset

Recently one superintendent was overheard saying, "Most of my employees are a pain in the neck. The problem is I can't run the course without them." That statement reflects the attitude that employees are a necessary evil. Fortunately, this is an extreme position.

Superintendents recognize that their employees are important; however, emphasis on interpersonal relationships is difficult. Most superintendents' training is in the physical sciences (horticultural sciences) where the importance of production technologies is continuously reinforced. In addition, most managers have trouble successfully managing the urgent tasks efficiently enough to leave sufficient time for the important, less urgent activities necessary for good interpersonal relationships.

A less common but more powerful attitude is that only people can utilize production technologies and physical assets to meet business goals. On a golf course this means that even the most modern production practices and most current technologies cannot enable you to exceed the golfers' expectations without the commitment of you and your staff. As discussed earlier, one expectation of employees is that they are recognized as important to the organization. Employees sense the real attitude of their supervisors toward them. Success in developing a committed, satisfied team of employees is dependent upon the realization that you and your staff are the most important asset of the golf course.

A Commitment to Providing Supporting Behaviors

When we think of supervising employees, the natural focus is on directing them to accomplish the required tasks: mowing the grass, fertilizing the greens, and raking the sand bunkers. As long as the golf course superintendent views the employee as someone who performs a series of tasks, employees will be carrying out a sequence of tasks while viewing them as a job.

Employee satisfaction comes from involvement, accomplishment, and growth. When the supervisor's only emphasis is on the task, completion of a task is simply a job done. When the employee recognizes the role the task plays in fulfilling the golfers' expectations, is committed to the goal, and is involved in designing the task, completion of the task results in job satisfaction. The difference between simply doing a job and job satisfaction results from the use of the supportive behaviors, including coaching, praising, supporting, and leading.

Blanchard, Zigarmi, and Zigarmi contrast supporting behavior with directive (task) behavior. "Three words can be used to define directive behavior: **structure, control,** and **supervise.** Different words are used to describe supportive behavior: **praise, listen,** and **facilitate**" (Blanchard, Zigarmi, and Zigarmi, 1985). They continue, "You support subordinates' efforts, listen to their suggestions and facilitate their interactions with others. And to build up their confidence and motivation you encourage and praise." Supporting behavior is much more interpersonal and developmental. Task behavior is usually urgent to job accomplishment; supportive behaviors are crucial to job commitment.

Supporting behaviors are important in managing golf course employees. They are used to communicate the vision the leadership of the golf course (board of directors, owners, golf course superintendents, golf pros) has for the course and to gain the commitment of the employees to that vision. Coaching, encouraging, praising, and reprimanding are then used to enable the now committed employee to maximize his or her contribution to the vision.

With the tremendous potential gain from supporting behavior, why do managers not use it more frequently? Three obstacles provide the answer. First, use of supporting behavior is not part of the traditional view of a supervisor. Second, use of supportive behavior is difficult for most managers with limited training in interpersonal skills and supervision. Third, even when we now recognize that supporting behavior is important, it is rarely urgent.

Overcoming the first two obstacles requires a commitment to using the supportive behaviors, and obtaining training in communication skills. In some situations, the supervision provided to the golf course superintendent by the green committee, course owner, or manager can serve as a role model. Overcoming the third obstacle is more difficult. Steven Covey says: "We react to urgent matters. Important matters that are not urgent require more initiative, more productivity. We must act to seize opportunity, to make things happen" (Covey, 1989). For most golf course superintendents to routinely and continuously have time for supporting behavior, a fundamental change in time management is required. This change means increased daily emphasis on important but not urgent activities, especially relationship building using supporting behaviors.

After supervisors attend a personnel management workshop, they usually increase their usage of supporting behaviors, but as time passes, use returns to its prior low level. This sequence results from the manager temporarily viewing the use of what was learned as urgent. Consequently, supportive behaviors are included with other urgent and important activities. As time passes, the urgency is lost and less time is devoted to supporting behaviors. Only if the manager has developed mechanisms to focus on important but not urgent activities can supporting behaviors be consistently utilized to develop a committed and motivated staff.

Continuing Personal Growth

The simplest way to summarize the objective of modern management is for you and your staff individually and collectively to be the best that you can be. The essential objective of every business is to use all of their physical production assets to their capacity. Modern human resource management has as its objective to develop and use all the capabilities of each member of the staff. Successful fulfillment of this objective leads to high productivity for the business and job satisfaction for the employees. For a golf course it leads to exceeding the golfers' expectations and to a satisfied, committed, happy staff.

For the golf course superintendent, who is both an employee and a supervisor, it leads to job satisfaction by fulfilling the expectations of the golfers and the green committee, and personal satisfaction through the achievements and growth of the staff.

Just as you must continually upgrade your knowledge on golf course production techniques and technologies, you must continually improve your ability to provide leadership to your course, supervise your staff, and optimally manage the course itself.

We suggest that you continue your management education in three areas:

1. Leadership and organizational development. This area increases your ability to provide leadership in the development of the golf course and its personnel. Chapters 2, 3, 9, and most of this chapter have focused on this area of management.
2. Supervisory skills. This area, focusing on supporting behaviors to supervise your staff, has been the major focus of this book.
3. Operational management. This includes the skills a golf course superintendent needs to effectively and efficiently plan and conduct the operational and tactical activities of the golf course. The last part of Chapter 2 and Chapter 4 focused on this area.

As you set goals and create a vision for the future of your course, be sure to place priority on training and development. This commitment to your personal education will help you to establish and maintain a reputation of excellence in golf course management.

References

Blanchard, K. and B. Tracey. 1989. Blanchard and Tracey on leadership. Blanchard Training and Development, Escondido, CA.

Blanchard, K., P. Zigarmi, and D. Zigarmi. 1985. Leadership and the one minute manager. William Morrow and Company, New York, NY.

Covey, S.R. 1989. The seven habits of highly effective people: Restoring the character ethic. Simon and Schuster, New York, NY.

Deming, W.E. 1986. Out of the crisis: Quality, productivity, and competitive position. Cambridge University Press, Cambridge, MA.

Franklin International Institute. 1989. Franklin day planner system: Guidebook. Franklin International Institute, Salt Lake City, UT.

National Golf Foundation. 1989. Golf consumer profile. National Golf Foundation, Jupiter, FL.

Tracey, B. 1986. The Psychology of Success. (audio cassette series).

Index